MATH

Grades 4 - 5

FRACTIONS
DECIMAL NUMBERS

✓ Fractions Concepts
✓ Mixed and Decimal Numbers
✓ Addition, Subtraction, Multiplication and Division with Fractions
✓ Decimal Numbers using Multiple Operations
✓ Fractions and Decimal Word Problems

101Minute.com

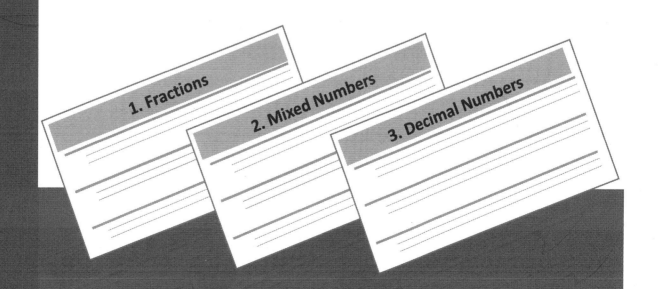

1. Fractions

2. Mixed Numbers

3. Decimal Numbers

About 101Minute.com

Welcome to 101Minute.com, a guide dedicated to help students excel academically.

We are focused on creating educational programs that help to enhance student's skills across various grades and subjects. Modules are designed per grade level that progressively enhances their skill and confidence each day.

Each subject category has several quizzes designed to assess student's mastery with the concept. By consistently devoting 101 minutes per week, students can demonstrate significant improvement.

We are committed to serving our student community by building effective tools and reward programs. We are open to receiving feedback on how we can improve to make this an even better experience for our students. Our goal is to create a fun and learning social educational environment for students, and reward them for their achievements.

Please visit us at 101Minute.com.

TABLE OF CONTENTS

1. FRACTIONS CONCEPT

1. Beth bought 6 lbs.' of apples. She used 1 lb. of apples to squeeze the juice in the evening. What fraction of the apples did she use for the juice?

2. There are 23 students in the 3rd grade. 2 were absent due to rain. What fraction of students is absent?

3. A pizza guy made 13 pizzas in an hour but he sold only 11 pizzas in an hour. What fraction of pizzas was sold in an hour?

4. A shopkeeper sold 13 of 15 TVs on black Friday. What fraction of TVs was sold on black Friday?

5. Robin brought a bag of marbles to his school. There were 7 red marbles out of 20 marbles. What fraction of Robins s marbles were red?

6. There are 23 compartments in a train. If there are 12 empty compartments what is fraction of empty compartments in the train?

7. There were 20 fish in an aquarium. 9 of them were dolphin. What fraction of the fish was dolphin?

8. Ram had 10 books on Math. Paul borrowed 3 books from him. What fraction of the books did he borrow?

9. Dora s father gave a pack of 8 chocolates to her on her birthday. She finished 5 chocolates within a week. What part of the pack did she finish within a week?

10. Mary s mom made homemade cookies on Christmas. She was able to make a total of 50 cookies. Out of 50 cookies 27 were chocolate chip cookies. What fraction of cookies was chocolate chip cookies?

11. Raman s parents brought a large pizza having 8 slices. If Raman ate 3 slices what portion of the pizza did he eat?

12. Ms. Alvis bought 8 apples and 9 oranges. What fraction of fruits is oranges?

13. Adam has 7 books of science and 5 books of math in his home library. What fraction of the books are math?

14. Greg s father gave him $20. Greg donated $11 to the church. What fraction of money did he donate to the church?

15. Rishi has 25 cards 8 of which are red and rest of them are blue. What fraction of cards are blue?

16. There were 24 crates of apples at a grocery store. Liz bought 5 crates of apples. What fraction of the apples did she buy?

17. Steve bought 2 dozen cupcakes. 7 of them were vanilla and rest of them were chocolate flavored. What fraction of cupcakes were vanilla flavored?

18. There are 13 boys and 12 girls in the 3rd grade. What fraction of the students is girls in the 3rd grade?

19. Gina bought 15 cupcakes from the bakery. She placed 8 cupcakes on the breakfast table. What fraction of cupcakes did she place on the table?

20. Karen's office is approx. 25 miles from his home. Due to traffic he covered only 13 miles in an hour. What fraction of distance is still remaining to reach office?

2. IDENTIFY EQUAL FRACTIONS

1. Which of the following fraction is equivalent to fraction 4/9?
   a) 8/18
   b) 4/18
   c) 8/9

2. Which of the following fraction is equivalent to fraction 2/11?
   a) 4/22
   b) 2/22
   c) 4/11

3. Which of the following fraction is equivalent to fraction 3/5?
   a) 9/15
   b) 9/5
   c) 12/20

4. Type the lowest possible fraction value for the fraction 12/20

5. Which of the following fraction is equivalent to fraction 4/9?
   a) 12/27
   b) 16/27
   c) 16/36

6. Which of the following fraction is equivalent to fraction 2/7?
   a) 6/21
   b) 9/21
   c) 8/28

7. Type the lowest possible fraction value for the fraction 8/44

8. Which of the following fraction is equivalent to fraction 3/5?
   a) 6/10
   b) 3/10
   c) 6/5

9. Type the lowest possible fraction value for the fraction 15/21

10. Which of the following fraction is equivalent to fraction 1/3?
    a) 3/9
    b) 9/3
    c) 4/12

11. Type the lowest possible fraction value for the fraction 4/12

12. Which of the following fraction is equivalent to fraction 3/7?
    a) 6/14
    b) 3/14
    c) 6/7

13. Type the lowest possible fraction value for the fraction 6/9

Copyright - 101Minute.com

14. Type the lowest possible fraction value for the fraction 9/21

15. Which of the following fraction is equivalent to fraction 5/9?
   a) 15/27
   b) 27/15
   c) 20/36

16. Type the lowest possible fraction value for the fraction 16/12

17. Type the lowest possible fraction value for the fraction 20/36

18. Which of the following fraction is equivalent to fraction 1/3?
   a) 2/6
   b) 1/6
   c) 2/3

19. Type the lowest possible fraction value for the fraction 12/27

20. Which of the following fraction is equivalent to fraction 5/7?
   a) 10/14
   b) 5/14
   c) 10/7

21. Which of the following fraction is equivalent to fraction 2/12?
   a) 1/6
   b) 6/1
   c) 8/4

22. Which of the following fraction is equivalent to fraction 3/7
   a) 9/21
   b) 21/9
   c) 12/28

23. Which of the following fraction is equivalent to fraction 5/9?
   a) 10/18
   b) 5/18
   c) 10/9

24. Which of the following fraction is equivalent to fraction 2/3?
   a) 6/9
   b) 2/6
   c) 4/3

25. Which of the following fraction is equivalent to fraction 2/7?
   a) 4/14
   b) 2/14
   c) 4/7

26. Which of the following fraction is equivalent to fraction 4/3?
    a) 8/6
    b) 4/6
    c) 8/3

27. Which of the following fraction is equivalent to fraction 5/7
    a) 15/21
    b) 21/15
    c) 20/28

28. Which of the following fraction is equivalent to fraction 2/3
    a) 4/6
    b) 2/6
    c) 4/3

29. Which of the following fraction is equivalent to fraction 4/3
    a) 12/9
    b) 12/90
    c) 16/12

30. Type the lowest possible fraction value for the fraction 6/21

Copyright - 101Minute.com

3. FRACTIONS (WORD PROBLEMS)

1. Melanie's mom made cakes on Christmas. She gave 3 4/9 servings of cake to her neighbor and 9 4/9 servings to her friends. How many servings of cake did she give?
   a) 12 8/9
   b) 3 8/9
   c) 9 8/9
   d) 6 8/9

2. If Sheila prepared 4/12 cup of soup and Monica prepared 5/12 cup, how much soup did they prepare in total?

3. Mira started to make vegetable soup. If her mom bought 2/9 kg of beans and 6/9 kg of lentils, how much ingredients do they have in total?

4. A mall has a big shopping complex and a move theatre. Rita spent 4 2/6 hours in shopping and another 5 3/6 hours watching movie before going home. How much time did they spend at the mall?
   a) 9 5/6
   b) 9 2/6
   c) 9 3/6
   d) 6 5/6

5. Gina needs 4/7 cups of water. If her mom already gave 1/7 cups of water to her, how much more water does she need?

6. In a farm, there are number of fruit trees, vegetable plants and other trees. If 3/10 of them are fruit trees and 5/10 are vegetable plants. What fraction of trees is neither fruit nor vegetables?

7. Sheila made a big pitcher of orange juice which can have 11 glasses. She gave 2 glasses to her younger brother and 3 glasses to her elder brother. What fraction of juice is left in the pitcher?

8. Mr. Chef served pasta, pizza and noodles on lunch. 1/4 of food was pasta. 2/4 of food was noodles. How much pizza was served on lunch?
   a) 1/4
   b) 2/4
   c) 3/4
   d) 4/4

9. There were 2 musical shows at Symphony Center. One musical show is 2/5 hours long and another musical show is also 2/5 hours long, how much time do you need to watch both musical shows?

10. Mr. David took a bus ride from his office to home. Bus fare is $3 per passenger. He gave $5 to the bus driver. What fraction of the money will bus driver return to Mr. David?

11. Gina needs 4/7 cups of water. If her mom already gave 1/7 cups of water to her, how much more water does she need?

12. Ms. Ramona have 13 girls and 15 boys in her class. 5 students didn't come to school because of rain. What fraction of the class was absent?

13. Jason bought 3 3/12 kg of apples and another 5/12 kg of oranges. How much fruits did he buy in total?
   a) 3 2/3
   b) 8/12
   c) 4 8/12
   d) 1 2/3

14. Mira started to make vegetable soup. If her mom bought 2/9 kg of beans and 6/9 kg of lentils, how much ingredients do they have in total?

15. Mrs. Alvin made a chocolate cake for her family cut it into 8 pieces. She gave 3 pieces to her neighbor. How much does she have left for her family?

16. Mike's office is 15 5/8 miles from his home. While returning from his office, he drove 6 3/8 miles then stopped to a restaurant to buy some food. How many more miles does he need to travel to reach home?
   a) 9 1/4
   b) 15 1/4
   c) 6 2/8
   d) 21 8/8

17. Elton drove from Chicago to New York. He covered 4/9 distance in 2 hours. How much distance is left to reach New York after 2 hours?

18. Mike's office is 15 5/8 miles from his home. While returning from his office, he drove 6 3/8 miles then stopped to a restaurant to buy some food. How many more miles does he need to travel to reach home?
   a) 9 1/4
   b) 15 2/8
   c) 6 2/8
   d) 21 1/4

19. Raman walked a total of 21 6/12 miles on Saturday and Sunday. If he walked 9 5/12 miles on Saturday. How many miles did he walk on Sunday?

20. Melanie's mom made cakes on Christmas. She gave 3 4/9 servings of cake to her neighbor and 9 4/9 servings to her friends. How many servings of cake did she give?

4. WRITE FRACTIONS IN ORDER

1. Match and put the fractions in the right order: 4/7, 4/5, 4/2

    4/5   is the smallest fraction.
    4/2   is the middle fraction.
    4/7   is the greatest fraction.

2. Are fractions 2/5, 2/7, 2/9 in the descending order?
    a) True
    b) False

3. Are fractions 3/4, 3/3, 3/2 in the ascending order?
    a) True
    b) False

4. Are fractions 3/2, 3/3, 3/4 in the descending order?
    a) True
    b) False

5. Are fractions 4/2, 4/3, 4/5 in the descending order?
    a) True
    b) False

6. Are fractions 2/9, 2/7, 2/5 in the ascending order?
    a) True
    b) False

7. Are fractions 5/6, 3/6, 1/6 in the descending order?
    a) True
    b) False

8. Are fractions 1/4, 3/4, 6/4 in the ascending order?
    a) True
    b) False

9. Are fractions 5/5, 5/4, 5/3 in the ascending order?
    a) True
    b) False

10. Are fractions 6/8, 7/8, 8/8 in the ascending order?
    a) True
    b) False

11. Are fractions 2/7, 3/7, 6/7 in the ascending order?
    a) True
    b) False

12. Match and put the fractions in the right order: 1/9, 3/9, 5/9
    3/9   is the smallest fraction.
    5/9   is the middle fraction.
    1/9   is the greatest fraction.

13. Match and put the fractions in the right order: 2/7, 2/6, 2/5

    2/6   is the smallest fraction.
    2/5   is the middle fraction.
    2/7   is the greatest fraction.

14. Match and put the fractions in the right order: 2/7, 3/7, 4/7

    3/7   is the smallest fraction.
    4/7   is the middle fraction.
    2/7   is the greatest fraction.

15. Are fractions 1/6, 3/6, 5/6 in the ascending order?
    a) True
    b) False

16. Are fractions 6/4, 3/4, 1/4 in the descending order?
    a) True
    b) False

17. Match and put the fractions in the right order: 1/5, 4/5, 5/5

    4/5   is the smallest fraction.
    5/5   is the middle fraction.
    1/5   is the greatest fraction.

18. Are fractions 5/5, 3/5, 2/5 in the descending order?
    a) True
    b) False

19. Match and put the fractions in the right order: 3/7, 3/6, 3/5

    3/6   is the smallest fraction.
    3/5   is the middle fraction.
    3/7   is the greatest fraction.

20. Are fractions 5/3, 5/4, 5/5 in the descending order?
    a) True
    b) False

21. Are fractions 8/8, 7/8, 6/8 in the descending order?
    a) True
    b) False

22. Are fractions 6/7, 6/8, 6/9 in the descending order?
    a) True
    b) False

23. Are fractions 2/5, 3/5, 5/5 in the ascending order?
    a) True
    b) False

24. Match and put the fractions in the right order: 3/8, 3/6, 3/4

    3/6   is the smallest fraction.
    3/4   is the middle fraction.
    3/8   is the greatest fraction.

25. Are fractions 4/5, 4/3, 4/2 in the ascending order?
    a) True
    b) False

26. Are fractions 1/4, 1/3, 1/2 in the ascending order?
    a) True
    b) False

27. Match and put the fractions in the right order: 2/10, 3/10, 4/10
    3/10   is the smallest fraction.
    4/10   is the middle fraction.
    2/10   is the greatest fraction.

28. Are fractions 6/7, 3/7, 2/7 in the descending order?
    a) True
    b) False

5. FIND THE SMALLEST AND LARGEST FRACTIONS

1. Find the smallest fraction in the following: 6/3, 17/2, 19/3
   - a) 17/2
   - b) 19/3
   - c) 6/3

2. Find the largest fraction in the following: 5/2, 13/8, 16/15

3. Find the smallest fraction in the following: 6/3, 17/2, 19/3
   - a) 17/2
   - b) 19/3
   - c) 6/3

4. Which is the smallest fraction? 7/2, 8/2 and 9/ 2

5. Find the smallest fraction in the following: 5/3, 6/4, 8/3
   - a) 6/4
   - b) 5/3
   - c) 8/3

6. Find the smallest fraction in the following: 19/2, 34/4, 54/3

7. Find the smallest fraction in the following: 4/3, 5/3, 6/5
   - a) 6/5
   - b) 4/3
   - c) 5/3

8. Find the smallest fraction in the following: 203/3, 204/4, 205/5

9. Find the largest fraction in the following: 1/2, 2/1, 3/1
   - a) 1/2
   - b) 3/1
   - c) 2/1

10. Find the smallest fraction in the following: 5/2, 13/8, 16/15

11. Find the smallest fraction in the following: 4/3, 5/3, 6/5
   - a) 6/5
   - b) 4/3
   - c) 5/3

12. Find the smallest fraction in the following: 1/2, 2/3, 3/4

13. Find the largest fraction in the following: 101/2, 102/2, 103/3

14. Find the smallest fraction in the following: 21/2, 31/2, 41/4

15. Which is the largest fraction? 7/2, 8/2 and 9/ 2

16. Find the smallest fraction in the following: 7/2, 17/6, 19/9
   a) 7/2
   b) 17/6
   c) 19/9

17. Find the largest fraction in the following: 21/2, 31/2, 41/4

18. Find the smallest fraction in the following: 11/3, 33/2, 17/7

19. Find the largest fraction in the following: 17/2, 35/4, 54/3

20. Which is the smallest fraction? 7/2, 8/2 and 9/ 2

21. Find the largest fraction in the following:3/2, 7/3, 8/6

22. Find the smallest fraction in the following: 1/2, 2/1, 3/1
   a) 2/1
   b) 1/2
   c) 3/1

23. Find the smallest fraction in the following: 7/2, 17/6, 19/9
   a) 7/2
   b) 17/6
   c) 19/9

24. Find the largest fraction in the following: 3/2, 7/3, 8/6

25. Find the largest fraction in the following: 21/2, 31/2, 41/4

26. Find the smallest fraction in the following: 203/3, 204/4, 205/5

27. Find the largest fraction in the following: 101/2, 102/2, 103/3

28. Find the largest fraction in the following: 5/2, 7/2, 9/2
   a) 7/2
   b) 9/2
   c) 5/2

29. Find the largest fraction in the following: /2, 7/3, 8/6

30. Find the largest fraction in the following:5/3, 6/4, 8/3
   a) 8/3
   b) 5/3
   c) 6/4

31. Find the largest fraction in the following: 5/2, 13/8, 16/15

32. Find the largest fraction in the following: 13/2, 17/2, 18/2

33. Find the largest fraction in the following: 1/2, 2/1, 3/1
   a) 1/2
   b) 3/1
   c) 2/1

34. Find the smallest fraction in the following: 101/2, 102/2, 103/3

35. Find the largest fraction in the following:
3/2, 4/3, 5/3
   a) 3/2
   b) 4/3
   c) 5/3

36. Find the largest fraction in the following: 5/2, 7/2, 9/2
   a) 7/2
   b) 9/2
   c) 5/2

37. Find the largest fraction in the following: 6/3, 17/2, 19/3
   a) 6/3
   b) 19/3
   c) 17/2

38. Find the largest fraction in the following: 4/3, 5/3, 6/5
   a) 4/3
   b) 5/3
   c) 6/5

39. Find the smallest fraction in the following: 19/2, 34/4, 54/3

40. Find the largest fraction in the following: 101/2, 102/2, 103/3

6. FRACTIONS PATTERNS AND SEQUENCE

1. Are the following in ascending order? 1/5, 1/10, 1/20
    a) False
    b) True

2. What would be the next fraction in the sequence? 2/17, 3/17, 4/17

3. What would be the next fraction in the sequence? 2/17, 4/17, 6/17

4. What would be the next fraction in the sequence? 10/20, 20/20, 30/20

5. What would be the next fraction in the sequence? 3/10, 5/10, 7/10,

6. Are the following in descending order? 1/2, 1/3, 1/5
    a) False
    b) True

7. Are the following in ascending order? 1/5, 1/10, 1/20
    a) False
    b) True

8. What would be the next fraction in the sequence? 3/11, 5/11, 7/11,

9. What would be the next fraction in the sequence? 2/17, 15/17, 28/17

10. What would be the next fraction in the sequence? 2/17, 5/17, 8/17

11. Are the following in ascending order? 17/7, 17/6, 17/5
    a) False
    b) True

12. Are the following in ascending order? 200/47, 200/46, 200/45
   a) False
   b) True

13. What would be the next fraction in the sequence? 100/20, 200/20, 300/20

14. Are the following in ascending order? 1/20, 1/10, 1/5
   a) False
   b) True

15. What would be the next fraction in the sequence? 3/10, 6/10, 9/10,

16. What would be the next fraction in the sequence? 3/10, 5/10, 7/10,

17. Are the following in descending order? 200/47, 200/46, 200/40
   a) False
   b) True

18. Are the following in ascending order? 200/47, 200/46, 200/45
   a) False
   b) True

19. Are the following in descending order? 17/7, 17/6, 17/3
   a) False
   b) True

20. Are the following in descending order? 1/2, 1/3, 1/5
   a) False
   b) True

7. ADD AND SUBTRACT SIMPLE FRACTIONS

Solve the following fractions equations:

1. $2/21 + 1/7 =$ _____

2. $3/32 - 1/16 =$ _____

3. $10/29 + 11/29 =$ _____

4. $12/41 - 11/41 =$ _____

5. $9/28 + 5/14 =$ _____

6. $8/37 - 7/37 =$ _____

7. $3/22 + 2/11 =$ _____

8. $2/31 + 3/31 =$ _____

9. $1/30 + 1/15 =$ _____

10. $4/33 - 1/11 =$ _____

11. $6/25 + 7/25 =$ _____

12. $5/24 + 1/4 =$ _____

13. $10/39 - 3/13 =$ _____

14. $7/36 - 1/6 =$ _____

15. $11/40 - 1/4 =$ _____

16. $1/20 + 1/10 =$ _____

17. $4/23 + 5/23 =$ _____

18. $9/38 - 4/19 =$ _____

19. $15/44 - 7/22 =$ _____

20. $6/35 - 1/7 =$ _____

21.   14/43 - 13/43 = _____

22.   5/34 - 2/17 = _____

23.   8/27 + 1/3 = _____

24.   7/26 + 4/13 = _____

25.   13/42 - 2/7 = _____

Copyright - 101Minute.com

8. FRACTIONS CONCEPT (MISSING NUMBERS)

Fill in the blanks:

1. 3/9 + 1/3 = _____

2. 2/4 = ___/2

3. 5/7 + 6/7 = _____

4. 1/4 + 1/8 + 1/16 + 1/16 = _____

5. 1/3 + 1/3 + 1/2 = _____

6. 1/5 + 1/5 + 2/10 + 1/5 = _____

7. 1/4 + 1/8 + 1/16 = _____

8. 1/2 + 1/4 + 1/8 = _____

9. 1/13 + 1/26 + 1/26 = _____

10. 1/13 + 1/26 = _____

11. 1/5 + 2/5 = _____

12. 2/7 + 3/7 + 3/7 + 3/7= _____

13. 1/5 + 1/5 + 2/10 = _____

14. 1/4 + 1/3 + 1/3 = _____

15. 400/2000 = 1/___

16. 1/2 + 1/2 + 1/2 = _____

17. 1/4 + 2/6 + 2/6= _____

18. 1/4 + 2/16 + 1/16 = _____

19. 9/18 + 1/9 = _____

20. 1/17 + 1/34 = _____

Copyright - 101Minute.com

21. $1/5 + 1/5 + 1/5 =$ _____

22. $500/2500 = 1/$___

23. $2/4 =$ ___$/2$

24. $1/3 + 1/3 + 1/3 =$ _____

25. $1/3 + 1/3 + 2/4 =$ _____

26. $1/4 + 1/8 + 1/16 + 1/16 =$ _____

27. $1/13 + 1/13 =$ _____

28. $1/4 + 1/8 =$ _____

29. $9/18 + 1/9 =$ _____

30. $4/8 + 2/4 + 1/2 =$ _____

31. $1/6 + 1/6 + 1/6 =$ _____

32. $1/5 + 1/5 + 1/5 + 1/5 =$ _____

33. $2/10 + 2/10 + 2/10 =$ _____

34. $1/2 + 1/2 + 3/2 =$ _____

35. $1/3 + 1/3 + 1/2 =$ _____

36. $7/6 + 7/9 + 1/3 =$ _____

37. $1/7 + 1/7 + 1/7 =$ _____

38. $1/5 + 1/5 + 1/5 =$ _____

39. $1/2 + 1 + 1 =$ _____

40. $1/4 + 1/8 + 1/16 + 1/16 =$ _____

9. COMPARE SIMPLE FRACTIONS

Compare and balance the following fraction equations using comparison sign > or = or <:

1. 2/4 _____ 1/4

2. 4/10 _____ 6/10

3. 2/4 _____ 2/4

4. 3/4 + 1/4 _____ 4/4

5. 4/5 _____ 5/5

6. 2/9 + 7/9 _____ 9/9

7. 2/9 + 2/9 _____ 9/9

8. 2/5 _____ 2/5

9. 1/7 _____ 1/7

10. 1/6 + 2/6 _____ 5/6

11. 5/7 _____ 2/7

12. 2/5 + 1/5 _____ 3/5

13. 3/7 _____ 5/7

14. 1/3 + 1/3 _____ 1/3

15. 2/6 + 3/6 _____ 5/6

16. 2/5 _____ 1/5

Copyright - 101Minute.com

17.   1/5 + 1/5 _____ 3/5

18.   4/6 + 2/6 _____ 3/6

19.   3/3 _____ 2/3

20.   2/5 + 1/5 _____ 2/5

21.   1/3 + 2/3 _____ 4/3

22.   2/6 _____ 2/6

23.   5/6 _____ 3/6

24.   2/4 + 1/4 _____ 1/4

25.   1/3 _____ 1/3

26.   1/4 + 1/4 _____ 4/4

27.   1/3 + 3/3 _____ 4/3

28.   1/9 _____ 2/9

29.   3/7 + 2/7 _____ 4/7

30.   5/9 _____ 8/9

Copyright - 101Minute.com

10. COMPARE NEGATIVE AND POSITIVE FRACTIONS

Compare the following fractions and place the right comparison sign > or = or <:

1. - 10/3 _____ - 11/3

2. - 5/7 _____ - 4/7

3. - 1/5 _____ - 2/5

4. 0 _____ 1/5

5. True or False: Zero is less than - 1/2
   a) False
   b) True

6. 5/1 _____ - 5

7. 5/1 _____ - 6

8. 7/200 _____ - 7/200

9. - 10/3 _____ - 11/3

10. True or False: Zero is less than 1/2
    a) False
    b) True

11. 2/1 _____ 1/2

12. 9/200 _____ - 9/200

13. - 20/20 _____ - 40/40

14. - 4/7 _____ - 16/7

15. 0 _____ - 1/2

16. - 2/3 _____ - 5/3

17. 0 _____ - 1/5

18. - 15/7 _____ - 15/ 7

Copyright - 101Minute.com

19. 2/5 _____ - 1/5

20. - 5/7 _____ - 4/7

21. 3/5 _____ - 1/5

22. 4/9 _____ 9/9

23. 1/9 _____ 9/9

24. 0 _____ - 1/2

25. 0 _____ - 10/1

26. 0 _____ - 1/5

27. - 2/3 _____ - 5/3

28. 0 _____ 1/5

29. 0 _____ 1/2

30. - 4/7 _____ - 6/7

31. 2/9 _____ 3/9

32. 1/9 _____ 3/9

33. - 20/20 _____ - 40/40

34. 4/5 _____ - 1/5

35. 0 _____ - 10/1

36. - 1/5 _____ - 2/5

37. - 5/7 _____ - 5/ 7

38. - 10 / 1 _____ - 1/10

39. - 10 / 1 _____ - 2/20

40. -1/2 _____ 1/2

11.   ADD AND SUBTRACT MIXED NUMBERS HAVING SAME DENOMINATORS

Add or subtract the following fractions equations as appropriate:

1. 3 1/3 + 2/3 = _____

2. 14/43 - 13/43 = _____

3. 3 2/3 - 3 1/3 = _____

4. 6/5 - 4/5 = _____

5. 2/3 + 5/3 = _____

6. 4/5 + 6/5 = _____

7. 1/20 + 1/10 = _____

8. 5/34 - 2/17 = _____

9. 4/3 - 1/3 = _____

10. 13/42 - 2/7 = _____

11. 5/24 + 1/4 = _____

12. 2 3/4 + 1 2/4 = _____

13. 2 2/5 + 1/5 = _____

14. 3/32 - 1/16 = _____

15. 3/4 - 2/4 = _____

16. 7/26 + 4/13 = _____

17. 1/30 + 1/15 = _____

18. 12/5 + 3/5 = _____

19. 15/44 - 7/22 = _____

20. 11/40 - 1/4 = _____

Copyright - **101Minute.com**

21. $3/4 + 5/4 =$ _____

22. $8/37 - 7/37 =$ _____

23. $9/38 - 4/19 =$ _____

24. $6\ 1/2 - 11/2 =$ _____

25. $9/28 + 5/14 =$ _____

26. $5/6 - 1/3 =$ _____

27. $3\ 1/3 - 4/3 =$ _____

28. $3/22 + 2/11 =$ _____

29. $4/3 + 1/3 =$ _____

30. $5 - 5/3 =$ _____

31. $2\ 3/4 - 9/4 =$ _____

32. $2/3 - 1/3 =$ _____

33. $8/27 + 1/3 =$ _____

34. $2/31 + 3/31 =$ _____

35. $9/4 + 11/4 =$ _____

36. $2/21 + 1/7 =$ _____

37. $4/33 - 1/11 =$ _____

38. $6/35 - 1/7 =$ _____

39. $1\ 4/5 + 3\ 1/5 =$ _____

40. $10/29 + 11/29 =$ _____

12.   ADD AND SUBTRACT MIXED NUMBERS

Solve the following fractions equations:

1. 2 3/32 - 1 2/16 = _____

2. 2 1/40 - 1 2/40 = _____

3. 1 3/41 - 1 1/41 = _____

4. 1 5/15 - 1 2/45 = _____

5. 3 3/32 - 2 1/32 = _____

6. 1 3/22 - 1 1/22 = _____

7. 2 1/12 - 1 2/36 = _____

8. 3 12/30 + 2 13/30 = _____

9. 1 3/20 - 1 2/40 = _____

10. 1 6/11 + 1 11/22 = _____

11. 1 4/7 + 1 1/14 = _____

12. 1 3/7 + 1 11/21 = _____

13. 3 1/12 - 2 1/36 = _____

14. 1 3/14 - 1 2/28 = _____

15. 5 6/13 + 4 11/13 = _____

16. 3 1/10 - 2 1/20 = _____

17. 1 1/12 - 1 1/18 = _____

18. 1 3/5 + 1 11/20 = _____

19. 2 1/5 + 2 11/25 = _____

20. 1 3/5 + 1 11/40 = _____

21. 1 4/9 + 1 1/18 = _____

22. 5 1/11 - 2 1/11 = _____

23. 1 12/25 + 2 11/25 = _____

24. 1 3/32 - 1 1/16 = _____

25. 1 1/10 + 1 2/30 = _____

Copyright - 101Minute.com

13.   ADD AND SUBTRACT FRACTIONS (TRUE OR FALSE)

Verify whether each of the following fractions statement is true or false?

1. Is 4/5 - 1/5 equal to 3/5
   a) False
   b) True

2. Is 4/3 + 1/3 equal to 4
   a) False
   b) True

3. Is 12/5 + 3/5 equal to 1/3
   a) False
   b) True

4. Is 4/3 - 1/3 equal to -1
   a) False
   b) True

5. Is 3/4 - 5/4 equal to -1/2
   a) True
   b) False

6. Is 13/3 - 11/3 equal to -2/3
   a) True
   b) False

7. Is 12/5 - 3/5 equal to 5/9
   a) False
   b) True

8. Is 9/4 - 11/4 equal to -1/2
   a) True
   b) False

9. Is 2/3 - 5/3 equal to -1
   a) True
   b) False

10. Is 13/2 - 11/2 equal to -1
    a) True
    b) False

11. Is 3/4 + 5/4 equal to 7/4
    a) True
    b) False

12. Is 3/4 + 2/4 equal to 5/4
    a) True
    b) False

13. Is 5/6 - 7/6 equal to -2/6
    a) True
    b) False

14. Is 4/5 - 6/5 equal to -2/5
    a) False
    b) True

15. Is 4/5 + 1/5 equal to 1
    a) False
    b) True

16. Is 9/4 + 11/4 equal to 5
    a) True
    b) False

17. Is 4/5 + 6/5 equal to 2
    a) False
    b) True

18. Is 10/3 + 4/3 equal to 14/3
    a) False
    b) True

19. Is 2/3 + 1/3 equal to 4/3
    a) True
    b) False

20. Is 12/5 + 1/5 equal to 13/5
    a) False
    b) True

21. Is 13/2 + 11/2 equal to 12
    a) False
    b) True

22. Is 2/3 + 5/3 equal to 7/3
    a) True
    b) False

23. Is 3/4 - 2/4 equal to 1/4
    a) True
    b) False

24. Is 2/3 - 1/3 equal to 2/3
    a) True
    b) False

25. Is 10/3 - 4/3 equal to 2
    a) False
    b) True

26. Is 12/5 - 1/5 equal to 11/5
    a) False
    b) True

27. Is 13/3 + 11/3 equal to 12/3
    a) True
    b) False

28. Is 5/6 + 7/6 equal to 7/3
    a) False
    b) True

14. ADD AND SUBTRACT UPTO 3 FRACTIONS HAVING SAME DENOMINATORS

Solve the following fractions equations:

1. $7/44 + 15/88 + 2/11 =$ _____

2. $8/49 + 17/98 + 9/49 =$ _____

3. $11/73 + 12/73 + 13/73 =$ _____

4. $1/14 + 3/28 + 1/7 =$ _____

5. $5/43 + 6/43 + 7/43 =$ _____

6. $4/29 + 9/58 + 5/29 =$ _____

7. $7/21 + 1/21 + 1/7 =$ _____

8. $5/34 + 11/68 + 3/17 =$ _____

9. $1/6 + 14/36 + 5/36 =$ _____

10. $1/2 + 1/4 - 4/8 + 2/8 =$ _____

11. $3/13 + 1/13 + 3/13 =$ _____

12. $13/83 + 14/83 + 15/83 =$ _____

13. $1/8 + 7/48 + 1/6 =$ _____

14. $2/19 + 5/38 + 3/19 =$ _____

15. $1/15 + 3/15 + 4/15 =$ _____

16. $7/41 + 7/41 + 8/41 =$ _____

Copyright - 101Minute.com

17. 1/81 + 30/81 + 12/81 = _____

22. 1/23 + 2/23 + 3/23 = _____

18. 1/11 + 4/33 + 5/33 = _____

23. 7/53 + 8/53 + 9/53 = _____

19. 9/24 + 2/24 + 2/24 = _____

24. 5/34 + 11/68 + 3/17 = _____

20. 5/31 + 16/93 + 17/93 = _____

25. 1/6 + 14/36 + 5/36 = _____

21. 1/7 + 10/63 + 11/63 = _____

15. ADD AND SUBTRACT UPTO 3 FRACTIONS HAVING DIFFERENT DENOMINATORS

Solve the following fractions equations:

1. $23/4 + 23/5 - 1/4 =$ _____

2. $1/5 + 11/3 - 1\ 1/5 =$ _____

3. $15/4 + 15/4 + 1\ 1/3 =$ _____

4. $12/15 + 6/15 + 1/3 =$ _____

5. $11/2 + 11/3 + 1\ 1/2 =$ _____

6. $2/3 + 6/5 + 1\ 1/3 =$ _____

7. $4/5 + 7/4 + 1/5 =$ _____

8. $6/7 + 8/9 + 1/7 =$ _____

9. $1/11 + 5/6 + 1/11 =$ _____

10. $4/5 + 7/8 + 1/5 =$ _____

11. $8/9 + 9/10 - 2\ 1/9 =$ _____

12. $3/4 + 3/5 + 1\ 1/4 =$ _____

13. $1/2 + 1/11 - 1\ 1/11 =$ _____

14. $5/6 + 5/7 + 1/6 =$ _____

15. $7/8 + 7/9 - 1/8 =$ _____

16. $16/7 + 8/9 - 1/7 =$ _____

Copyright - 101Minute.com

17. 13/4 + 13/5 + 1/4 = _____

18. 1/11 + 5/6 + 3 1/11 = _____

19. 23/4 + 1 23/5 - 1/4 = _____

20. 3 1/5 + 11/3 - 2 1/5 = _____

21. 15/4 + 15/4 + 4 1/3 = ___

22. 12/15 + 6/15 + 1 1/3 = _____

23. 1 11/2 + 1 11/3 + 1 1/2 = _____

24. 1 2/3 + 1 6/5 + 2 1/3 = _____

25. 1 4/5 + 7/4 + 1/5 = _____

Copyright - 101Minute.com

16. ADD AND SUBTRACT UP TO 3 FRACTIONS AND MIXED NUMBERS HAVING SAME DENOMINATORS (WORD PROBLEMS)

1. Andy took 7/16 hours to clean up the room and then played for 13/16 hours and spent 9/16 hrs. arranging his clothes. How much did Andy spend all together?

2. Jose played for 3/7 hours on computer and then watched TV for 11/14 hours and 4/7 hrs. on computer after a break again. How much time did he spend playing on computer and watching TV together?

3. John took 1/3 minutes to solve the first puzzle and then 1/2 minutes to solve second puzzle and 2/3 for another puzzle. How long did it take to solve 3 puzzles?

4. Josh played for 11/24 hours on computer, 7/8 hrs. on Game Box and then played outside for 3/5 hours. How much did he play?

5. Susan played for 6/13 hours on Sunday morning, 23/26 hours on Sunday evening and played for 7/13 hours on Saturday. How much did he play over the weekend?

6. John did Math for 13/28 hours, and spent 15/28 hours on writing. He also did reading for 25/28 hours over the weekend. How much time did he spend on study on weekend?

Copyright - 101Minute.com

7. Samuel played on his computer for 11/23 hours, Game Box for 17/46 hrs. and then studied for 12/23 hours. How much time did Samuel play and study overall?

8. Tim walks 1/5 miles and then jogs for 2/5 miles and then walks 3/5 miles again. How many miles did he travel overall?

9. Joseph spent 4/9 hours. cleaning and 5/6 hours playing cards and 5/9 hours on his computer. How much time did she spend cleaning and playing?

10. Alisha walks 3/8 miles to school and then walks 5/8 miles from school to playground and 5/8 miles back to home every day. How many miles does she walk every day?

11. John had a balance of 17/36 million dollars in his bank account and he deposited 11/12 million more and then he withdrew 19/36 million dollars from bank. What will be his balance now?

12. Raman played for 9/20 hrs. and then studied for 17/20 hrs. and then played for 11/20 hrs. after a break. How much time did he spend playing and studying together?

13. Joseph studied for 7/15 hrs. on Sunday morning, 9/10 hrs. on Sunday evening and then studied 8/15 hours on Saturday. How much did she study over weekend?

14. Jeff plays on computer for 2/5 hours and then plays on Game Box for 7/10 hours and then again on computer for 3/5 hrs. How long did he play?

15.   Richard played for 5/12 hours on computer and then watched TV for 3/4 hours and then plays for 7/12 hrs. How much time did he spend playing and TV?

16.   Andy did Math for 13/28 hours, 15/28 hrs. on writing and reading for 25/28 hours on Sunday. How much did he study together on Sunday?

17.   Rachel played on Game Box for 23/48 hrs. and 15/16 hrs. on computer and studied for only 25/48 hrs. on Sunday. How much extra did Rachel play on Sunday as compared to studies?

18.   Sam played on computer for 8/17 hrs. and Game Box for 31/34 hrs. and Asha played for 9/17 hours. How much extra did Sam play compare to Asha?

19.   Sam ate 15/32 pizza, John ate 29/32 pizza and Asha ate 17/32 pizza. How much more pizza did Sam and John eat together compared to Asha?

20.   Shop owner spent 5/11 hrs. arranging the vegetables and 19/22 hrs. arranging the fruits and 6/11 hrs. arranging baskets. How long did he spend for arranging shop together?

17.   ADD AND SUBTRACT FRACTIONS (WORD PROBLEMS)

1.   Lisa ate 2/3 pizza and John ate 1/3 pizza. How much more pizza did Lisa eat than John?

2.   A shop keeper spent 6 1/2 hrs. arranging the vegetables and 5 1/2 hrs. arranging the fruits. How much time did he spend for arranging vegetables and fruits?

3.   Joseph spent 3 1/3 hrs. cleaning his house and 1 1/3 hours playing outside. How much time in total did he spend in both cleaning and playing?

4.   Ramona travelled 2 2/5 miles north on her new bike and then travelled 3/5 miles south. How far is she from the starting point?

5.   Jeff played on his computer for 2/3 hours and then played on Game Box for 5/3 hours. How long did he play?

6.   Andrew took 2 1/4 hours to read his new book and spend another 2 3/4 hours to complete his homework. How much time did he spend in reading and completing his homework?

7.   Rachel played for 2 2/5 hrs. and studied for only 1/5 hrs. on Sunday. How much extra time did Rachel spend on playing than studying?

8.   Rick played for 4/5 hours on his computer and then watched TV for 6/5 hours. How much time did he spend on computer and TV?

9.   Susan played for 4 1/3 hours on Saturday and played for 3 2/3 hours on Sunday. How much did he play over the weekend?

10.   Tim ran 1/4 miles and then walked for 2/3 miles. How many total miles did he travel?

11.   Leon travelled 1 1/3 miles north and then travelled back 1/3 miles south. How many miles is he from the starting point?

12.   John took 3/4 minutes to solve first puzzle and 1 7/16 minutes to solve the second puzzle. How long did he take to solve both puzzles?

13.   Andrew spent 2/3 hours on Math homework and 1/3 hours on English homework. How much time did he spend to complete his homework?

14.   A shopkeeper spent 6 1/2 to setup his shop and 5 1/2 hrs. to sell things to his customer after the setup on grand opening of his shop. How much time did he spend more on setting up the shop than selling on first day?

15.   Tom ate 3/4 pizza and Usha ate 1/2 pizza. How much extra pizza did Tom eat than Usha?

16. Josh played baseball for 2 2/5 hours and played basketball for 3/5 hours. How many hours did he play in total?

17. Alisha walks 5/6 miles to her friend's house and walks another 7/6 miles to her school with her friend. How many miles does she walk to her school?

18. From starting point A, Mike travelled 3 1/3 miles east to point B. From point B, he travelled back 3 2/3 miles west. How many miles is he away from the starting point A?

19. Sam played for 4/5 hrs. and Usha played for 1/5 hours. How much extra did Sam play than Usha?

20. Samuel played for 3 1/3 hours and then studied for 4/3 hours. How much extra did Samuel play compare to his studies?

21. Joseph studied for 4/3 hrs. on Saturday and studied 1/3 hours on Sunday. How much did he study over the weekend?

22. John is a rich person. He had 5/6 million dollars in his bank account. He withdrew 1/6 million dollars from his bank account on Friday. What is the remaining balance in his bank account?

23. Raman played for 1/5 hrs. and studied for 2 2/5 hours on Friday. How much time did he spend on both playing and studying on Friday?

24. Mike played for 3/4 hours on computer and watched TV for 5/4 hours. How much time did Mike spend on computer and TV?

18.   SIMPLE FRACTIONS (MIXED PROBLEMS)

1.   Mike went on trekking for 2 miles. While coming back, he took a shorter route and walked 1/2 of the distance to come back home. How much distance did you walk all together?

2.   Greg's dad is 1/2 of the age of his grandpa. If his age is 1/4 of his dad and he is 10 years old. What is his grandpa's age?

3.   Lisa's age is 1/3rd the age of her mom. What is the age of Lisa's mom if she is 20 years old?

4.   Richard walked around 2/3 mile. If his school is 1 mile from home how many he is away from his school?

5.   Shyam gave 1/3 of cookies to his sister Susan and 1/3 of cookies to his sister Julie. How much cookies did he give to his sisters?

6.   If you already walked around 1/3 mile and your school is 1 mile from your home. How much distance is remaining now?

7.   If you have eaten 1/3 of cookies. How much is it remaining?

8.   You walked 2/3 miles from Spiderman ride to Batman ride, and then you walked 1/6 mile from batman ride to Water Mountain ride. How much distance did you walk in total?

9. Sam is 1/4 age of his dad. If his dad is 40 years what is Sam's age?

10. A box had lot of mangoes. 1/3 of the mangoes in the box were sour. If there were 30 mangoes in the box, how many were not sour?

11. Mary has a little lamb and a big lamb. Height of little lamb is 1/3 of big lamb. If big lamb s 60 inches tall how much tall is little lamb?

19. MULTIPLY FRACTIONS AND WHOLE NUMBERS (TRUE OR FALSE)

Verify whether each of the following fractions equations is correct (true) or not (false)

1. 19/40 x 7 = 3 13/40
    a) True
    b) False

2. 4/9 x 8 = 3 5/9
    a) False
    b) True

3. 23/48 x 11 = 5 13/50
    a) True
    b) False

4. 9/20 x 9 = 4 1/20
    a) False
    b) True

5. 12/25 x 12 = 5 19/50
    a) True
    b) False

6. 7/15 x 5 = 2 4/5
    a) False
    b) True

7. 11/23 x 10 = 4 18/23
    a) False
    b) True

8. 1/3 x 2 = 2/3
    a) False
    b) True

9. 8/17 x 8 = 3 13/17
    a) False
    b) True

10. 21/44 x 9 = 4 13/44
    a) True
    b) False

11. 13/28 x 6 = 2 9/28
    a) True
    b) False

12. 9/19 x 6 = 2 16/19
    a) True
    b) False

13. 3/8 x 4 = 1 1/8
    a) False
    b) True

14. 7/16 x 7 = 3 1/16
    a) True
    b) False

15. $6/13 \times 3 = 1\ 11/13$
   a) True
   b) False

16. $25/52 \times 13 = 7\ 1/4$
   a) False
   b) True

17. $11/24 \times 4 = 1\ \ 3/8$
   a) False
   b) True

18. $23/48 \times 11 = 5\ 13/48$
   a) False
   b) True

19. $15/32 \times 7 = 3\ \ 9/32$
   a) True
   b) False

20. $17/36 \times 5 = 2\ 13/36$
   a) True
   b) False

21. $25/52 \times 13 = 6\ \ 1/8$
   a) False
   b) True

22. $2/5 \times 4 = 1\ \ 3/5$
   a) True
   b) False

23. $3/7 \times 6 = 2\ \ 4/7$
   a) False
   b) True

24. $12/25 \times 23 = 5\ 19/25$
   a) True
   b) False

25. $5/12 \times 5 = 2\ \ 1/12$
   a) True
   b) False

26. $5/11 \times 10 = 4\ \ 6/11$
False
True

27. $1/4 \times 1 = 1/4$
   a) True
   b) False

28. $10/21 \times 8 = 3\ 17/21$
   a) False
   b) True

Copyright - 101Minute.com

20. MULTIPLY FRACTIONS BY WHOLE 1 OR 2 DIGIT NUMBERS

Solve the following fractions equations:

1. 9/20 x 5 = _____

2. 11/24 x 45 = _____

3. 17/36 x 15 = _____

4. 3/8 x 10 = _____

5. 1/4 x 5 = _____

6. 23/48 x 10 = _____

7. 25/52 x 5 = _____

8. 9/19 x 10 = _____

9. 7/16 x 9 = _____

10. 2/5 x 10 = _____

11. 8/17 x 20 = _____

12. 5/12 x 20 = _____

13. 5/11 x 50 = _____

14. 19/40 x 5 = _____

15. 15/32 x 25 = _____

16. 11/23 x 15 = _____

Copyright - 101Minute.com

17. 12/25 x 5 = _____

18. 3/7 x 20 = _____

19. 6/13 x 40 = _____

20. 4/9 x 9 = _____

21. 1/3 x 5 = _____

22. 13/28 x 35 = _____

23. 7/15 x 30 = _____

24. 21/44 x 20 = _____

25. 10/21 x 25 = _____

Copyright - 101Minute.com

21.   COMPARE AND BALANCE PRODUCT OF TWO FRACTIONS

Verify whether each of the following fractions expression is correct (true) or not (false)

1. 13/45 x 2/5 = 26/225
    a) False
    b) True

2. 1 2/5 x 1 9/10 = 2 33/50
    a) False
    b) True

3. 5 1/5 x 6 1/5 = 32 6/25
    a) False
    b) True

4. 9/20 x 7/10 < 61/2000
    a) True
    b) False

5. 1 2/5 x 1 13/20 > 2 101/100
    a) True
    b) False

6. 16/25 x 21/25 < 331/745
    a) True
    b) False

7. 5/9 x 2/3 = 10/27
    a) True
    b) False

8. 6/7 x 1 1/7 < 48/51
    a) False
    b) True

9. 34/65 x 44/65 > 92/231
    a) True
    b) False

10. 1/2 x 1 = 1/2
    a) True
    b) False

11. 1 2/5 x 1 11/15 = 2 32/75
    a) True
    b) False

12. 44/45 x 1 1/5 = 1 13/75
    a) True
    b) False

13. 11/30 x 8/15 = 44/225
    a) True
    b) False

14. 1 3/55 x 1 11/55 > 1 24/19
    a) False
    b) True

15. 23/30 x 14/15 = 161/225
    a) True
    b) False

16. 4/9 x 2/3 = 8/27
    a) False
    b) True

17. 1 2/5 x 1 13/20 < 2 1/100
    a) True
    b) False

18. 9/20 x 23/40 > 102/800
    a) False
    b) True

19. 2 4/25 x 2 14/25 = 5 331/625
    a) False
    b) True

20. 1 2/5 x 1 23/20 = 2 33/100
    a) True
    b) False

21. 7/15 x 4/5 = 27/75
    a) False
    b) True

22. 8/25 x 34/75 = 75/517
    a) False
    b) True

23. 4/11 x 5/11 = 20/121
    a) False
    b) True

24. 2/5 x 48/95 = 96/475
    a) True
    b) False

25. 16/35 x 26/35 = 217/639
    a) True
    b) False

26. 16/25 x 58/75 = 293/592
    a) False
    b) True

27. 1 2/5 x 1 13/20 = 2 32/100
    a) False
    b) True

28. 12/25 x 22/25 = 264/625
    a) False
    b) True

22. COMPARE FRACTIONS WITH WHOLE NUMBER (TRUE OR FALSE)

Verify whether following equations are correct(true) or incorrect(false):

1. Is 1/4 + 2/4 + 3/4 > 1
   a) True
   b) False

2. Is 2/5 + 1/5 + 1/5 > 1
   a) False
   b) True

3. Is 1/4 + 2/4 + 3/4 = 1
   a) False
   b) True

4. Is 1/7 + 2/7 + 7/7 < 1
   a) False
   b) True

5. Is 3/4 + 1/4 = 1
   a) True
   b) False

6. Is 1/7 + 2/7 + 4/7 = 1
   True
   False

7. Is 1/7 + 2/7 + 7/7 = 1
   False
   True

8. Is 2/5 > 3/5
   a) False
   b) True

9. Is 2/9 + 9/9 > 1
   a) True
   b) False

10. Is 1/4 + 2/4 + 1/4 > 1
    a) False
    b) True

11. Is 3/6 + 2/6 = 1
    a) False
    b) True

12. Is 4/5 + 4/5 = 1
    a) False
    b) True

13. Is 3/6 + 3/6 = 1
    a) True
    b) False

14. Is 2/5 > 1/5
    a) True
    b) False

15. Is 3/8 > 3/8
   a) False
   b) True

16. Is 1/4 > 2/4
   a) False
   b) True

17. Is 3/8 + 3/8 + 1/8 < 1
   a) True
   b) False

18. Is 2/4 > 1/4
   a) True
   b) False

19. Is 2/9 < 7/9
   a) True
   b) False

20. Is 2/9 + 7/9 > 1
   a) False
   b) True

21. Is 2/9 + 7/9 = 1
   a) True
   b) False

22. Is 2/6 < 3/6
   a) True
   b) False

23. Is 1/3 + 2/3 = 1
   a) False
   b) True

24. Is 3/4 + 2/4 = 1
   a) False
   b) True

25. Is 2/9 + 9/9 = 1
   a) False
   b) True

26. Is 3/5 + 1/5 < 1
   a) True
   b) False

27. Is 3/9 + 3/9 + 3/9 < 1
   a) False
   b) True

28. Is 1/3 + 4/3 > 1
   a) True
   b) False

29. Is 4/7 > 2/7
   a) False
   b) True

30. Is 2/5 + 1/5 + 2/5 = 1
   a) True
   b) False

31. Is 3/8 + 3/8 + 2/8 = 1
   a) True
   b) False

32. Is 2/4 + 1/4 < 1
   a) True
   b) False

33. Is 3/9 + 3/9 + 6/9 = 1
   a) False
   b) True

34. Is 3/4 + 1/4 < 1
   a) False
   b) True

35. Is 3/8 + 3/8 + 2/8 < 1
   a) False
   b) True

36. Is 1/3 < 2/3
   a) True
   b) False

37. Is 3/6 + 3/6 < 1
   a) True
   b) False

38. Is 3/6 + 3/6 < 1
   a) False
   b) True

39. Is 1/5 < 4/5
   a) True
   b) False

40. Is 4/5 + 1/5 = 1
   a) True
   b) False

23.	MULTIPLY 2 FRACTIONS

Solve the following fractions equations:

1. 1 1/4 x 4 7/8 =

2. 1 5/17 x 4 7/17 =

3. 1 1/5 x 5 2/5 =

4. 1 5/14 x 3 3/4 =

5. 1 5/13 x 3 6/13 =

6. 1 5/21 x 5 =

7. 1 5/25 x 5 5/8 =

8. 1 5/16 x 4 7/32 =

9. 1 5/22 x 5 5/44 =

10. 1 5/29 x 5 20/29 =

11. 1 5/7 x 2 1/7 =

12. 1 5/3 x 5 5/3 =

13. 1 5/12 x 3 1/8 =

14. 1 5/6 x 2 1/12 =

15. 1 5/16 x 5 25/3 =

16. 1 5/18 x 4 7/12 =

Copyright - 101Minute.com

17. 1 4/25 x 5 5/16 =

18. 1 1/2 x 2 1/4 =

19. 1 5/11 x 2 8/11 =

20. 2 x 1/2 =

21. 1 5/8 x 2 3/16 =

22. 1 5/9 x 4 2/3 =

23. 1 1/3 x 4 =

24. 1 5/2 x 5 5/9 =

25. 1 5/9 x 2 2/9 =

24.   MULTIPLY 2 FRACTIONS (TRUE OR FALSE)

Verify whether each of the following fractions expression is correct (true) or not (false)

1. 1 2/5 x 1 13/20 = 2 32/100
    a) False
    b) True

2. 2/5 x 48/95 = 96/475
    a) True
    b) False

3. 4/11 x 5/11 = 20/121
    a) False
    b) True

4. 1 2/5 x 1 13/20 = 2 33/100
    a) True
    b) False

5. 1 2/5 x 1 9/10 = 2 33/50
    a) False
    b) True

6. 6/7 x 1 1/7 = 48/51
    a) False
    b) True

7. 1 2/5 x 1 13/20 = 2 31/100
    a) True
    b) False

8. 11/30 x 8/15 = 44/225
    a) True
    b) False

9. 13/45 x 2/5 = 26/225
    a) False
    b) True

10. 16/25 x 58/75 = 293/592
    a) False
    b) True

11. 5 1/5 x 6 1/5 = 32 6/25
    a) False
    b) True

12. 7/15 x 4/5 = 27/75
    a) False
    b) True

13. 12/25 x 22/25 = 264/625
    a) False
    b) True

14. 16/35 x 26/35 = 217/639
    a) True
    b) False

15. 1 2/5 x 1 13/20 = 2 33/100
  a) True
  b) False

16. 1/2 x 1 = 1/2
  a) True
  b) False

17. 1 3/55 x 1 11/55 = 1 24/79
  a) False
  b) True

18. 9/20 x 23/40 = 203/800
  a) False
  b) True

19. 9/20 x 7/10 = 61/200
  a) True
  b) False

20. 16/25 x 21/25 = 331/625
  a) True
  b) False

21. 1 2/5 x 1 11/15 = 2 32/75
  a) True
  b) False

22. 23/30 x 14/15 = 161/225
  a) True
  b) False

23. 4/9 x 2/3 = 8/27
  a) False
  b) True

24. 5/9 x 2/3 = 10/27
  a) True
  b) False

25. 44/45 x 1 1/5 = 1 13/75
  a) True
  b) False

26. 8/25 x 34/75 = 75/517
  a) False
  b) True

27. 34/65 x 44/65 = 92/257
  a) True
  b) False

28. 2 4/25 x 2 14/25 = 5 331/625
  a) False
  b) True

25. MULTIPLY FRACTIONS (WORD PROBLEMS)

1. If Tom walks 17/36 miles in a day. How much will he walk in 15 days?

2. A robot covered 13/28 miles in an hour. How much will it cover in 35 hrs.?

3. There are 5 kids in a party. Each kid eats approximate 1/4 pizza. How much pizza will they eat in total?

4. There are 10 kids in a birthday party. Each kid eats 2/5 pizza approximately. How much pizza we should order for the birthday party?

5. In a relay race of 30 robots, each robot covered 7/15 mile. What is the total distance covered by 30 robots?

6. A pre-school teacher is going to give juice to the kids during the break. Each kid gets 11/24 liters of juice. There are 45 total kids. How much juice does the teacher need for all the kids?

7. If Cindy can complete 1/3rd of the painting in one sitting. How much painting will be done over 3 sittings?

8. 3/7 oz. of silver is required to make one electronics chip. How much silver is required to make 20 chips?

9. Usha takes 15/32 hrs. to complete 1 painting. How many hrs. does she need to complete 25 paintings?

10. A boy drinks 9/20 oz. of milk in a day. How much milk will he drink over weekdays in a week?

11. Lisa walks 6/13 miles every day. How many miles in total will she walk in 40 days?

12. A rich man decided to donate some gold to various Churches in his county last Christmas. He donated 5/12 oz. gold to each Church. If there are 20 Churches in his country, how much gold did he donate on Christmas?

13. If Tom walks 3/8 miles in a day. How many miles he will over 10 days?

14. John's dad walks 7/16 miles to his work every day. How many total miles will he walk to work over 9 days?

15. A student got 5/11 of a pizza in his school party. How many pizzas are needed for 50 students?

16. John's mom needs 4/9 hour to cook a single dish for a dinner party. If there are 9 dishes in a party. How much time did she spend to cook the dinner?

17. There are 10 walls to be painted in a house. Mike needs 9/19 hour to paint a single wall. How many hours does he need to paint all 10 walls?

26.   MULTIPLY UP TO 3 FRACTIONS AND ANSWER IN MIXED NUMBER

Solve the following fractions equations:

1. 3/4 x 7 3/4 x 1/2 = _____

2. 1 x 3 1/8 x 1/2 = _____

3. 2 1/2 x 3/4 x 1/2 = _____

4. 1/2 x 1/2 x 1/2 = _____

5. 1 x 21 1/2 x 1/2 = _____

6. 2 1/2 x 4 1/2 x 1/2 = _____

7. 2/3 x 5 1/2 x 1/2 = _____

8. 2 1/2 x 7/8 x 1/2 = _____

9. 3/4 x 11 1/4 x 1/2 = _____

10. 2 1/2 x 9 1/2 x 1/2 = _____

11. 5/8 x 4 3/8 x 1/2 = _____

12. 1 1/2 x 5 1/4 x 1/2 = _____

13. 1/10 x 2 7/10 x 1/2 = _____

14. 1 x 14 1/2 x 1/2 = _____

15. 3/2 x 1 7/8 x 1/2 = _____

16. 1/3 x 1/3 x 1/2 = _____

Copyright - 101Minute.com

17. 3/5 x 3 7/10 x 1/37 = _____

18. 5/8 x 6 1/8 x 1/2 = _____

19. 2 1/2 x 1/2 x 1/2 = _____

20. 2/5 x 1 7/10 x 5/2 = _____

21. 7/12 x 3 1/4 x 4/7 = _____

22. 2 1/2 x 5/6 x 1/2 = _____

23. 1 1/6 x 3 5/6 x 1/2 = _____

24. 2/3 x 7 5/6 x 1/2 = _____

25. 1 1/2 x 2 3/4 x 1/2 = _____

27.   DIVIDE FRACTIONS – FRACTION BY FRACTION

Solve the following fractions equations:

1.   5/16 is divided by 3/8 = ___

2.   1/30 is divided by 1/15 = ___

3.   1/48 is divided by 1/24 = ___

4.   3/22 is divided by 2/11 = ___

5.   1/9 is divided by 5/36 = ___

6.   3/14 is divided by 1/4 = ___

7.   3/34 is divided by 2/17 = ___

8.   1/8 is divided by 1/4 = ___

9.   1/5 is divided by 3/10 = ___

10.   3/52 is divided by 1/13 = ___

11.   3/20 is divided by 7/40 = ___

12.   1/25 is divided by 3/50 = ___

13.   1/18 is divided by 1/9 = ___

14.   5/56 is divided by 3/28 = ___

15.   2/7 is divided by 5/14 = ___

16.   1/16 is divided by 1/32 = ___

Copyright - 101Minute.com

17. 5/38 is divided by 3/19 = ___   22. 1/10 is divided by 3/20 = ___

18. 1/4 is divided by 1/3 = ___   23. 5/26 is divided by 3/13 = ___

19. 1/6 is divided by 5/24 = ___   24. 9/46 is divided by 5/23 = ___

20. 1/6 is divided by 4/21 = ___   25. 2/27 is divided by 5/54 = ___

21. 2/11 is divided by 9/44 = ___

28.   DIVIDE FRACTIONS – FRACTIONS AND WHOLE NUMBER

Solve the following fractions equations:

1. 1/2 is divided by 3 = ___

2. 4 is divided by 1/3 = ___

3. 1/4 is divided by 3 = ___

4. 1/3 is divided by 3 = ___

5. 1/3 is divided by 11 = ___

6. 4 is divided by 1/5 = 4/5
    a) True
    b) False

7. 4 is divided by 1/3 = ___

8. 1/4 is divided by 3 = ___

9. 1/6 is divided by 3 = ___

10. 1/5 is divided by 3 = ___

11. 5 is divided by 1/4 = ___

12. 6 is divided by 1/6 = 1
    a) False
    b) True

13. 1/6 is divided by 3 = ___

14. 1/6 is divided by 11 = ___

15. 5 is divided by 1/3 = ___

16. 5 is divided by 1/3 = 15
    a) False
    b) True

17. 7 is divided by 1/6 = ___

18. 6 is divided by 1/3 = 18
    a) True
    b) False

19. 4 is divided by 1/5 = ___

20. 6 is divided by 1/2 = ___

21. 1/2 is divided by 3 = ___

22. 7 is divided by 1/3 = 7/3
    a) False
    b) True

23. 1/3 is divided by 3 = ___

24. 1/6 is divided by 3 = ___

25. 7 is divided by 1/6 = ___

26. 1/2 is divided by 12 = ___

27. 1/5 is divided by 10 = ___

28. 7 is divided by 1/2 = 7/2
    a) True
    b) False

29. 1/5 is divided by 3 = ___

30. 1/3 is divided by 3 = ___

31. 3 is divided by 1/2 = 6
    a) True
    b) False

32. 6 is divided by 1/2 = 12
    a) False
    b) True

33. 5 is divided by 1/6 = ___

34. 1/5 is divided by 3 = ___

35. 3 is divided by 1/2 = 6
    a) True
    b) False

36. 4 is divided by 1/2 = 8
    a) False
    b) True

37. 1/5 is divided by 10 = ___

38.　7 is divided by 1/5 = ___

39.　7 is divided by 1/3 = ___

40.　1/3 is divided by 3 = ___

29.   COMPARE FRACTIONS DIVISION (TRUE OR FALSE)

Verify each of the following fractions equations whether it is correct (true) or not (false):

1.   1/25 is divided by 3/50 > 1
     a) False
     b) True

2.   2/11 is divided by 9/44 > 8/9
     a) False
     b) True

3.   1/9 is divided by 5/36 = 4/5
     a) False
     b) True

4.   1/8 is divided by 1/4 = 1/2
     a) False
     b) True

5.   5/38 is divided by 3/19 = 5/6
     a) False
     b) True

6.   3/34 is divided by 2/17 = 3/4
     a) False
     b) True

7.   3/22 is divided by 2/11 = 3/4
     a) False
     b) True

8.   1/16 is divided by 1/32 = 2
     a) False
     b) True

9.   1/6 is divided by 5/24 = 4/5
     a) False
     b) True

10.   3/52 is divided by 1/13 = 3/4
      a) False
      b) True

11.   2/27 is divided by 5/54 < 4/5
      a) False
      b) True

12.   3/14 is divided by 1/4 = 6/7
      a) False
      b) True

13.   1/30 is divided by 1/15 = 1/2
      a) False
      b) True

14.   1/5 is divided by 3/10 = 2/3
      a) False
      b) True

15. 5/56 is divided by 3/28 = 5/6
   a) False
   b) True

16. 1/4 is divided by 1/3 = 3/4
   a) False
   b) True

17. 1/18 is divided by 1/9 = 1/2
   a) False
   b) True

18. 3/20 is divided by 7/40 > 6/7
   a) False
   b) True

19. 1/6 is divided by 4/21 < 7/8
   a) False
   b) True

20. 9/46 is divided by 5/23 > 19/10
   a) False
   b) True

21. 5/26 is divided by 3/13 = 5/6
   a) False
   b) True

22. 1/48 is divided by 1/24 = 1/2
   a) False
   b) True

23. 2/7 is divided by 5/14 = 4/5
   a) False
   b) True

24. 1/10 is divided by 3/20 = 2/3
   a) False
   b) True

25. 5/16 is divided by 3/8 = 5/6
   a) False
   b) True

30. DIVIDE FRACTIONS (TRUE OR FALSE)

Verify each of the following fractions equations whether it is correct (true) or not (false):

1. 5 is divided by 1/2 = 10
   a) True
   b) False

2. 7 is divided by 1/4 = 7/4
   a) False
   b) True

3. 5 is divided by 1/3 = 15
   a) False
   b) True

4. 6 is divided by 1/6 = 1
   a) False
   b) True

5. 7 is divided by 1/5 = 7/5
   a) True
   b) False

6. 3 is divided by 1/4 = 3/4
   a) False
   b) True

7. 5 is divided by 1/4 = 20
   a) False
   b) True

8. 4 is divided by 1/4 = 16
   a) False
   b) True

9. 3 is divided by 1/6 = 1/2
   a) True
   b) False

10. 4 is divided by 1/4 = 16
    a) False
    b) True

11. 6 is divided by 1/2 = 12
    a) False
    b) True

12. 4 is divided by 1/2 = 8
    a) False
    b) True

13. 7 is divided by 1/2 = 7/2
    a) True
    b) False

14. 5 is divided by 1/5 = 25
    a) True
    b) False

15. 6 is divided by 1/6 = 1
   a) False
   b) True

16. 7 is divided by 1/6 = 7/6
   a) False
   b) True

17. 6 is divided by 1/5 = 6/5
   a) True
   b) False

18. 6 is divided by 1/2 = 12
   a) False
   b) True

19. 4 is divided by 1/5 = 4/5
   a) True
   b) False

20. 6 is divided by 1/5 = 6/5
   a) True
   b) False

21. 4 is divided by 1/5 = 4/5
   a) True
   b) False

22. 3 is divided by 1/4 = 3/4
   a) False
   b) True

23. 5 is divided by 1/5 = 25
   True
   False

24. 7 is divided by 1/3 = 7/3
   a) False
   b) True

25. 4 is divided by 1/2 = 8
   False
   True

26. 3 is divided by 1/6 = 1/2
   a) True
   b) False

27. 7 is divided by 1/4 = 7/4
   a) False
   b) True

28. 4 is divided by 1/3 = 12/1
   a) True
   b) False

29. 5 is divided by 1/6 = 5/6
   a) False
   b) True

30. 5 is divided by 1/6 = 5/6
   a) False
   b) True

Copyright - 101Minute.com

31. 7 is divided by 1/2 = 7/2
  a) True
  b) False

32. 4 is divided by 1/6 = 6/4
  a) True
  b) False

33. 3 is divided by 1/5 = 3/5
  a) False
  b) True

34. 6 is divided by 1/4 = 24
  a) True
  b) False

35. 7 is divided by 1/3 = 7/3
  a) False
  b) True

36. 4 is divided by 1/6 = 6/4
  a) True
  b) False

37. 3 is divided by 1/2 = 6
  a) True
  b) False

38. 6 is divided by 1/3 = 18
  a) True
  b) False

39. 3 is divided by 1/5 = 3/5
  a) False
  b) True

40. 7 is divided by 1/5 = 7/5
  a) True
  b) False

31. DIVIDE WHOLE NUMBERS BY FRACTIONS

Solve the following fractions equations:

1. 4 is divided by 1/2 = ___

2. 6 is divided by 1/3 = ___

3. 6 is divided by 1/6 = ___

4. 4 is divided by 1/5 = ___

5. 7 is divided by 1/4 = ___

6. 6 is divided by 1/4 = ___

7. 6 is divided by 1/5 = ___

8. 4 is divided by 1/3 = ___

9. 7 is divided by 1/2 = ___

10. 6 is divided by 1/2 = ___

11. 6 is divided by 1/6 = ___

12. 7 is divided by 1/4 = ___

13. 4 is divided by 1/5 = ___

14. 4 is divided by 1/4 = ___

15. 3 is divided by 1/3 = ___

16. 6 is divided by 1/4 = ___

17. 3 is divided by 1/4 = ___

18. 3 is divided by 1/5 = ___

19. 5 is divided by 1/5 = ___

20. 4 is divided by 1/6 = ___

21. 7 is divided by 1/6 = ___

22. 5 is divided by 1/2 = ___

23. 5 is divided by 1/4 = ___

24. 3 is divided by 1/3 = ___

25. 3 is divided by 1/6 = ___

26. 4 is divided by 1/4 = ___

27. 3 is divided by 1/2 = ___

28. 4 is divided by 1/2 = ___

29. 5 is divided by 1/6 = ___

30. 4 is divided by 1/3 = ___

31. 5 is divided by 1/6 = ___

32. 5 is divided by 1/5 = ___

33. 5 is divided by 1/3 = ___

34. 6 is divided by 1/2 = ___

35. 6 is divided by 1/3 = ___

36. 7 is divided by 1/2 = ___

37. 5 is divided by 1/4 = ___

38. 4 is divided by 1/6 = ___

39. 7 is divided by 1/6 = ___

40. 3 is divided by 1/5 = ___

32.   DIVIDE WHOLE NUMBERS BY MIXED NUMBER

Solve and choose the right answer for the following fractions equations:

1. 3 is divided by 5 5/23 = ___
    a) 1 17/23
    b) 23/40

2. 4 is divided by 5 5/16 = ___
    a) 1 21/64
    b) 64/85

3. 3 is divided by 5 20/29 = ___
    a) 1 26/29
    b) 29/55

4. 5 is divided by 4 14/19 = ___
    a) 1 1/18
    b) 18/19

5. 2 is divided by 5 5/44 = ___
    a) 1 49/88
    b) 2 88/225

6. 4 is divided by 2 = ___
    a) 2
    b) 1/2

7. 6 is divided by 5 25/52 = ___
    a) 95/104
    b) 1 9/95

8. 5 is divided by 2 3/16 = ___
    a) 2 2/7
    b) 7/16

9. 4 is divided by 4 7/12 = ___
    a) 48/55
    b) 7/48

10. 5 is divided by 3 3/4 = ___
    a) 1 1/3
    b) 3/4

11. 6 is divided by 4 7/8 = ___
    a) 1 3/13
    b) 13/16

12. 2 is divided by 2 8/11 = ___
    a) 11/15
    b) 1 4/11

13. 3 is divided by 4 7/17 = ___
    a) 17/25
    b) 1 8/17

14. 1 is divided by 2 1/4 = ___
    a) 4/9
    b) 2 1/4

Copyright - 101Minute.com

15.   6 is divided by 2   2/9 = ___
   a)   2   7/10
   b)   10/27

21.   3 is divided by 3   1/8 = ___
   a)   24/25
   b)   1 1/24

16.   2 is divided by 4   7/32 = ___
   a)   64/135
   b)   2   7/64

22.   5 is divided by 5   2/5 = ___
   a)   1 2/25
   b)   25/27

17.   4 is divided by 2   1/7 = ___
   a)   1 13/15
   b)   15/28

23.   1 is divided by 5   5/9 = ___
   a)   5   5/9
   b)   9/50

18.   1 is divided by 5   = ___
   a)   1/5
   b)   5

24.   4 is divided by 3   6/13 = ___
   a)   1 7/45
   b)   45/52

19.   2 is divided by 5   5/8 = ___
   a)   2 13/16
   b)   16/45

25.   1 is divided by 4   = ___
   a)   1/4
   b)   4

20.   3 is divided by 2   1/12 = ___
   a)   1 11/25
   b)   25/36

33.   DIVIDE FRACTIONS (WORD PROBLEMS)

1.   Josh wants to divide 5 chocolate packets by giving 1/3 of a packet to each kid. To how many kids he can distribute the chlorates?

2.   Rita ordered 3 pizzas and wanted to divide 1/2 of a pizza to each of her kids. To how many kids she would be able to give the pizzas?

3.   Mike donated 7 bags of rice to homeless families during Christmas. How many families will receive the rice if each one of them receives 1/2 of a bag?

4.   Lisa has 6 pack of candies. How many kids will receive candies if 1/3 of a pack is given to each kid?

5.   John has 2 pizzas. How much pizza will each kid receive if there are 6 kids?

6.   Anne has 5 chocolate packets. How many kids will receive chocolate if 1/5 packet is given to a kid?

7.   John has 2 pizzas. How much pizza will each kid receive if there are 6 kids?

8.   Greg has 3 packs of cookies. How many kids will get cookies if 1/5 of a packet is given to 1 kid?

9. Divide 5 papers is such a manner that each kid gets 1/5th of a paper to make a small paper flower. How many kids will get a piece of paper if it is fully distributed?

10. Tom has 5 bags of mangos. How many people will receive some mangoes if 1/5th of a bag to each person?

11. 3 liters of juice is equally distributed among school children during lunch break. If each child gets 1/3 liter of water. How many children will be get the juice?

12. A chef prepared 4 big bowls of soup and served 1/5th of a bowl of each of his customer in a small cup. How many customers can he serve?

13. Josh got a contract to construct 5 miles of a highway in 3 phases, and he can construct 1/3rd of a mile in a day. How many days does he need to construct the road?

14. There were 4 marbles in a red box. If you gave 1 marble to each of your friend. Then what fraction of marbles did you give to each of your friends?

15. There are 16 candies in a blue packet. If you gave 4 candies to 1 person. What fraction of candies did you give to him?

16. Divide 5 gallons' juice among players so that each player gets 1/4 gallons of juice. How many players can be served with 5 gallons of juice?

17. Divide 5 pizzas so that each kid gets 1/2 pizza. How many kids can be served with 5 pizzas?

18. Mom cooked 3 pizzas and gave 1/2 of a pizza each to her kids. How many kids will get pizza?

19. There are 100 candies in a candy bag. If you donated 25 candies. What fraction of the candies have you donated?

20. Divide 5 gallons' juice among players so that each player gets 1/6 gallons of juice. How many players can be served with 5 gallons of juice?

34. CONVERSION BETWEEN DECIMAL AND FRACTION

Convert between decimal and fraction as appropriate:

1. Convert decimal to fraction: 1.45

2. Convert decimal to fraction: 1.14

3. Convert fraction to decimal: 3 9/20

4. Convert decimal to fraction: 0.74

5. Convert fraction to decimal: 1 17/20

6. Convert fraction to decimal: 2 9/20

7. Convert decimal to fraction: 0.85

8. Convert decimal to fraction: 1.94

9. Convert decimal to fraction: 1.74

10. Convert decimal to fraction: 1.54

11. Convert fraction to decimal: 2 1/4

12. Convert decimal to fraction: 0.45

13. Convert fraction to decimal: 3 13/20

14. Convert fraction to decimal: 4 1/20

15. Convert fraction to decimal: 3 1/20

16. Convert decimal to fraction: 1.05

17. Convert decimal to fraction: 0.34

18. Convert decimal to fraction: 2.14

19. Convert decimal to fraction: 1.34

20. Convert fraction to decimal: 4 1/4

21. Convert decimal to fraction: 0.54

22. Convert decimal to fraction: 0.65

23. Convert fraction to decimal: 3 17/20

24. Convert fraction to decimal: 3 1/4

25. Convert decimal to fraction: 1.25

26. Convert fraction to decimal: 2 13/20

27. Convert decimal to fraction: 0.94

28. Convert decimal to fraction: 1.65

29. Convert fraction to decimal: 2 1/20

30. Convert fraction to decimal: 2 17/20

35.   ROUNDING OF DECIMAL NUMBERS

Round off the following numbers as stated below:

1.   Round off 0.804347826086957 to thousandths

2.   Round off 4.47169811320755 to hundredths

3.   Round off 0.125 to hundredths

4.   Round off 0.0256410256410256 to hundredths

5.   Round off 1.60714285714286 to hundredths

6.   Round off 0.116279069767442 to hundredths

7.   Round off 0.666666666666667 to tenths

8.   Round off 1.76190476190476 to hundredths

9.   Round off 4.001 to hundredths

10.   Round off 0.0423728813559322 to thousandths

11.   Round off 0.36734693877551 to thousandths

12.   Round off 0.0454545454545455 to thousandths

Copyright - 101Minute.com

13.   Round off 1.74436090225564 to thousandths

14.   Round off 0.442477876106195 to thousandths

15.   Round off 0.436893203883495 to thousandths

16.   Round off 0.307692307692308 to tenths

17.   Round off 1.8515625 to thousandths

18.   Round off 1.56521739130435 to hundredths

19.   Round off 3.26470588235294 to hundredths

20.   Round off 0.333333333333333 to tenths

21.   Round off 0.354838709677419 to thousandths

22.   Round off 0.036144578313253 to thousandths

23.   Round off 1.83333333333333 to tenths

24.   Round off 1.55244755244755 to thousandths

25.   Round off 1.39393939393939 to hundredths

26.   Round off 0.0487804878048781 to thousandths

27. Round off 0.375 to tenths

28. Round off 0.425925925925926 to thousandths

29. Round off 0.0136986301369863 to hundredths

30. Round off 1.31578947368421 to hundredths

Copyright - 101Minute.com

36.   COMPARE AND BALANCE EQUATIONS HAVING DECIMAL NUMBERS AND FRACTIONS

Verify whether each of the following fractions expression is correct (true) or not (false)

1. 4.5 + 1 1/2 = 6
    a) False
    b) True

2. 4.5 + 6 1/4 > 10 3/4
    a) False
    b) True

3. 1 + 1/2 = 1 1/2
    a) False
    b) True

4. 3.5 + 1 3/4 = 5 1/4
    a) False
    b) True

5. 2.5 + 1 1/4 > 3 3/4
    a) False
    b) True

6. 4 + 3 3/4 = 7 3/4
    a) False
    b) True

7. 0.5 + 1/4 = 3/4
    a) False
    b) True

8. 3.5 + 5 3/4 > 9 1/4
    a) False
    b) True

9. 3.5 + 3 1/2 = 7
    a) False
    b) True

10. 2.5 + 3 = 5 1/2
    a) False
    b) True

11. 4.5 + 5 1/2   <> 10
    a) False
    b) True

12. 5 + 4 1/4 = 9 1/4
    a) False
    b) True

13. 1 + 4 1/2 = 5 1/2
    a) False
    b) True

14. 6.5 + 7 1/4 < 13 3/4
    a) False
    b) True

Copyright - 101Minute.com

15. 1.5 + 3/4 = 2 1/4
   a) False
   b) True

23. 3 + 3 1/4 = 6 1/4
   a) False
   b) True

16. 1.5 + 1 1/2 = 3
   a) False
   b) True

24. 3.5 + 3 1/2 = 7
   a) False
   b) True

17. 5.5 + 7 1/2   > 13
   a) False
   b) True

25. 5 + 6 1/2 > 11 1/2
   a) False
   b) True

18. 3 + 1 1/2 = 4 1/2
   a) False
   b) True

26. 5.5 + 6 3/4 < 12 1/4
   a) False
   b) True

19. 1 + 2 1/4 = 3 1/4
   a) False
   b) True

27. 2.5 + 5 1/4 = 7 3/4
   a) False
   b) True

20. 4.5 + 4 = 8 1/2
   a) False
   b) True

28. 1.5 + 2 1/2 = 4
   a) False
   b) True

21. 1.5 + 4 3/4 = 6 1/4
   a) False
   b) True

29. 3 + 5 1/2 < 8 1/2
   a) False
   b) True

22. 2 + 2 3/4 = 4 3/4
   a) False
   b) True

37. DECIMAL NUMBERS PROBLEMS (TRUE OR FALSE)

Verify whether each of the following fractions expression is correct (true) or not (false)

1. Fraction equivalent of 1.34 is 1 17/50
   a) True
   b) False

2. Fraction equivalent of 0.45 is 9/20
   a) True
   b) False

3. Decimal equivalent of 3 13/20 is 3.75
   a) True
   b) False

4. Fraction equivalent of 0.74 is 37/50
   a) True
   b) False

5. Decimal equivalent of 1 17/20 is 1.85
   a) True
   b) False

6. Fraction equivalent of 0.94 is 47/50
   a) True
   b) False

7. Fraction equivalent of 1.05 is 1 1/20
   a) True
   b) False

8. Decimal equivalent of 2 13/20 is 2.75
   a) True
   b) False

9. Fraction equivalent of 0.34 is 17/50
   a) True
   b) False

10. Decimal equivalent of 3 1/4 is 3.5
    a) True
    b) False

11. Fraction equivalent of 1.74 is 1 37/50
    a) True
    b) False

12. Fraction equivalent of 1.54 is 1 27/50
    a) True
    b) False

13. Fraction equivalent of 0.54 is 27/50
    a) True
    b) False

14. Fraction equivalent of 1.94 is 1 47/50
    a) True
    b) False

15. Decimal equivalent of 3 17/20 is 3.05
    a) True
    b) False

16. Decimal equivalent of 2 1/20 is 2.05
    a) True
    b) False

17. Decimal equivalent of 4 1/20 is 4.15
    a) True
    b) False

18. Fraction equivalent of 2.14 is 2 7/50
    a) True
    b) False

19. Fraction equivalent of 1.14 is 1 7/50
    a) True
    b) False

20. Fraction equivalent of 1.45 is 1 9/20
    a) True
    b) False

21. Decimal equivalent of 2 1/4 is 2.25
    a) True
    b) False

22. Fraction equivalent of 0.65 is 13/20
    a) True
    b) False

23. Decimal equivalent of 2 17/20 is 2.65
    a) True
    b) False

24. Decimal equivalent of 2 9/20 is 2.45
    a) True
    b) False

25. Fraction equivalent of 1.25 is 1 1/4
    a) True
    b) False

26. Decimal equivalent of 3 1/20 is 3.25
    a) True
    b) False

27. Decimal equivalent of 3 9/20 is 3.6
    a) True
    b) False

28. Fraction equivalent of 1.65 is 1 13/20
    a) True
    b) False

29. Fraction equivalent of 0.85 is 17/20
    a) True
    b) False

Copyright - 101Minute.com

38.   DECIMAL NUMBERS PROBLEMS (WORD PROBLEMS)

1.   School lunches cost $10.00 per week. About how much would 10 weeks of lunches cost?

2.   Andrew ran for a total of 190.6 miles in practice over 41.5 days. About how many miles did he average per day?

3.   Lisa earns $11.75 per hour for gardening. If she worked 22 hours this month, then how much did she earn?

4.   Joseph earns $11.75 per hour for gardening. If he worked 33.2 hours this month, then how much did he earn?

5.   Andrew will pay for his new car in 36 monthly payments. If his car loan is for $25,061 then how much will Mike pay each month? Round your answer to nearest cent.

6.   A pizza costs $4 per slice. If there are 2 kids and both wants one pizza slice, then how much will have to spend together?

7.   A store owner has 9.21 lbs. of candy. If she puts the candy into 10 jars, how much candy will each jar contain?

8. A member of the school track team ran for a total of 189.6 miles in practice over 51.5 days. About how many miles did he average per day?

9. A store owner has 19.21 lbs. of candy. If she puts the candy into 10 jars, how much candy will each jar contain?

10. John's car costs $40,000 and Lisa's car costs $20,000. If they have to buy the cars together how much they have to spend the money to but both the cars?

11. Alex earns $11.50 per hour for gardening. If she worked 2 hours this week, then how much did she earn?

12. Mike will pay for his new car in 48 monthly payments. If his car loan is for $21,061, then how much will Mike pay each month? Round your answer to nearest cent.

13. Jason's car costs $30,000 and Greg's car costs $10,000. If they have to buy the cars together how much they have to spend the money?

14. Eisha's car gives 30 miles per gallon on the highway. If her car's fuel tank holds 11.5 gallons, then how far can she travel on one full tank of gas?

15. John's car gets 30 miles per gallon on the highway. If his fuel tank holds 12 gallons, then how far can he travel on one full tank of gas?

16. Alexandra earns $11.25 per hour for gardening. If she worked 2 hours this week, then how much did she earn?

17. School lunches cost $10.75 per week. About how much would 10 weeks of lunches cost?

18. A pizza costs $4 per slice. If there are 3 kids and all 3 of them wants one pizza slice, then how much they have to spend together?

39.	ADD DECIMAL NUMBERS

Add the following decimal numbers:

1. 141715.37 + 62667.69 = _____

11. 341025.75 + 149270.45 = _____

2. 131225.35 + 58109.65 = _____

12. 503621.06 + 219920.07 = _____

3. 293820.66 + 128759.27 = _____

13. 36815.17 + 17087.29 = _____

4. 393475.85 + 172060.65 = _____

14. 362005.79 + 158386.53 = _____

5. 288575.65 + 126480.25 = _____

15. 445925.95 + 194850.85 = _____

6. 409210.88 + 178897.71 = _____

16. 257105.59 + 112806.13 = _____

7. 183675.45 + 80899.85 = _____

17. 508866.07 + 222199.09 = _____

8. 309555.69 + 135596.33 = _____

18. 204655.49 + 90015.93 = _____

9. 89265.27 + 39877.49 = _____

19. 94510.28 + 42156.51 = _____

10. 451170.96 + 197129.87 = _____

20. 414455.89 + 181176.73 = _____

21. 31570.16 + 14808.27 = _____

22. 194165.47 + 85457.89 = _____

23. 403965.87 + 176618.69 = _____

24. 514111.08 + 224478.11 = _____

25. 461660.98 + 201687.91 = _____

26. 466905.99 + 203966.93 = _____

27. 47305.19 + 21645.33 = _____

28. 456415.97 + 199408.89 = _____

29. 146960.38 + 64946.71 = _____

30. 246615.57 + 108248.09 = _____

31. 251860.58 + 110527.11 = _____

32. 84020.26 + 37598.47 = _____

33. 42060.18 + 19366.31 = _____

34. 136470.36 + 60388.67 = _____

35. 346270.76 + 151549.47 = _____

36. 398720.86 + 174339.67 = _____

37. 519356.09 + 226757.13 = _____

38. 236125.55 + 103690.05 = _____

39. 199410.48 + 87736.91 = _____

40. 304310.68 + 133317.31 = _____

40.   SUBTRACT DECIMAL NUMBERS

Subtract the following decimal numbers:

1.   375916.71 - 294697.56 = _____

2.   409605.03 - 321177.96 = _____

3.   123254.31 - 96094.56 = _____

4.   329595.27 - 258287.01 = _____

5.   119043.27 - 92784.51 = _____

6.   72721.83 - 56373.96 = _____

7.   418027.11 - 327798.06 = _____

8.   194841.99 - 152365.41 = _____

9.   249585.51 - 195396.06 = _____

10.   22189.35 - 16653.36 = _____

11.   333806.31 - 261597.06 = _____

12.   371705.67 - 291387.51 = _____

13.   359072.55 - 281457.36 = _____

14.   30611.43 - 23273.46 = _____

15.   207475.11 - 162295.56 = _____

16.   283273.83 - 221876.46 = _____

17.   363283.59 - 284767.41 = _____

18.   152731.59 - 119264.91 = _____

19.   279062.79 - 218566.41 = _____

20.   64299.75 - 49753.86 = _____

Copyright - 101Minute.com

21. 81143.91 - 62994.06 = _____

22. 367494.63 - 288077.46 = _____

23. 148520.55 - 115954.86 = _____

24. 114832.23 - 89474.46 = _____

25. 110621.19 - 86164.41 = _____

26. 161153.67 - 125885.01 = _____

27. 236952.39 - 185465.91 = _____

28. 39033.51 - 29893.56 = _____

29. 156942.63 - 122574.96 = _____

30. 190630.95 - 149055.36 = _____

31. 232741.35 - 182155.86 = _____

32. 34822.47 - 26583.51 = _____

33. 287484.87 - 225186.51 = _____

34. 316962.15 - 248356.86 = _____

35. 203264.07 - 158985.51 = _____

36. 76932.87 - 59684.01 = _____

37. 165364.71 - 129195.06 = _____

38. 321173.19 - 251666.91 = _____

39. 199053.03 - 155675.46 = _____

40. 241163.43 - 188775.96 = _____

Copyright - 101Minute.com

41.   MULTIPLE OPERATIONS USING DECIMAL NUMBERS

Solve the following equations:

1. (76.48 - 17.24) /4= _____

2. 2 x (42.67 - 32.21) = _____

3. 7 x (97.75 - 20.33) = _____

4. 7 x (48.12 + 13.12) = _____

5. 66.79 - 26.85 + 10.03 = _____

6. 76.35 + 83.94 - 28.94 = _____

7. 114.59 + 72.3 - 24.58 = _____

8. 4 x (76.48 + 17.24) = _____

9. (55.21 + 14.15) /8= _____

10. (33.94 - 11.02) /5= _____

11. 57.23 + 89.76 - 31.12 = _____

12. 57.23 + 19.76 - 21.12 = _____

13. (62.3 - 15.18) /2= _____

14. 105.03 + 75.21 - 25.67 = _____

15. 47.67 - 12.67 + 32.21 = _____

16. 152.83 + 90.66 - 19.3 = _____

17. 6 x (41.03 - 12.09) = _____

18. (12.67 + 32.21) /2= _____

19. 4 x (26.85 - 10.03) = _____

20. 3 x (19.76 + 21.12) = _____

Copyright - 101Minute.com

21. (19.76 - 11.12) /3= _____

22. 143.27 - 83.57 + 18.27 = _____

23. 5 x (83.57 + 18.27) = _____

24. 95.47 + 78.12 - 26.76 = _____

25. 4 x (26.85 + 10.03) = _____

26. (76.48 + 17.24) /4= _____

27. (55.21 - 14.15) /8= _____

28. 76.35 + 33.94 - 11.06 = _____

29. (83.57 - 18.27) /5= _____

30. 133.71 + 66.48 - 22.4 = _____

31. (97.75 - 20.33) /7= _____

32. 133.71 + 76.48 - 17.24 = _____

33. 5 x (33.94 + 11.02) = _____

34. 2 x (62.3 - 15.18) = _____

35. 105.03 - 55.21 + 14.15 = _____

36. 85.91 + 81.03 - 27.85 = _____

37. 85.91 - 41.03 + 12.09 = _____

38. 8 x (55.21 - 14.15) = _____

39. 95.47 + 48.12 - 13.12 = _____

40. 8 x (55.21 + 14.15) = _____

42. ADD AND SUBTRACT THREE DECIMAL NUMBERS

Add the following numbers up to 1 decimal place:

1. 33.1 + 28.3 + 16.6 = _____

2. 77.1 + 62.3 - 38.6 = _____

3. 52.9 + 43.6 - 26.5 = _____

4. 68.3 + 55.5 - 34.2 = _____

5. 79.3 + 64 - 39.7 = _____

6. 41.9 + 35.1 - 2.3 = _____

7. 72.7 + 58.9 - 36.4 = _____

8. 81.5 + 65.7 - 41.9 = _____

9. 44.1 + 36.8 + 22.1 = _____

10. 35.3 + 30 - 17.7 = _____

11. 55.1 + 45.3 - 27.6 = _____

12. 61.7 + 50.4 + 32 = _____

13. 57.3 + 47 - 28.7 = _____

14. 6.7 + 7.9 + 30.9 = _____

15. 33.1 + 28.3 - 16.6 = _____

16. 63.9 + 52.1 + 3.4 = _____

17. 39.7 + 33.4 - 19.9 = _____

18. 30.9 + 26.6 + 15.5 = _____

19. 46.3 + 38.5 + 23.2 = _____

20. 63.9 + 52.1 - 3.4 = _____

Copyright - 101Minute.com

21.   48.5 + 40.2 - 24.3 = _____

22.   79.3 + 64 + 39.7 = _____

23.   4.5 + 6.2 - 21 = _____

24.   8.9 + 9.6 - 40.8 = _____

25.   44.1 + 36.8 - 22.1 = _____

26.   13.3 + 13 - 6.7 = _____

27.   81.5 + 65.7 + 41.9 = _____

28.   22.1 + 19.8 + 11.1 = _____

29.   66.1 + 53.8 - 33.1 = _____

30.   41.9 + 35.1 + 2.3 = _____

31.   19.9 + 18.1 - 0.5 = _____

32.   6.7 + 7.9 - 30.9 = _____

33.   70.5 + 57.2 + 35.3 = _____

34.   77.1 + 62.3 + 38.6 = _____

35.   8.9 + 9.6 + 40.8 = _____

36.   83.7 + 67.4 + 43 = _____

37.   4.5 + 6.2 + 21 = _____

38.   59.5 + 48.7 - 29.8 = _____

39.   13.3 + 13 + 6.7 = _____

40.   59.5 + 48.7 + 29.8 = _____

Copyright - 101Minute.com

43.   ADD AND SUBTRACT DECIMAL NUMBERS (TRUE OR FALSE)

Verify whether each of the following addition is correct (true) or not (false)

1. 27.79 + 35.32 + 8.11 = 101.22
    a) False
    b) True

2. Is 38.91 + 49.08 + 12.55 = 110.54
    a) False
    b) True

3. Is 50.03 + 62.84 + 16.99 = 149.86
    a) False
    b) True

4. Is 25.01 + 31.88 = 56.89
    a) True
    b) False

5. Is 19.45 + 25 = 74.45
    a) False
    b) True

6. Is 50.03 + 62.84 = 132.87
    a) False
    b) True

7. Is 47.25 + 59.4 + 15.88 = 122.53
    a) True
    b) False

8. Is 25.01 + 31.88 - 7 = 49.89
    a) True
    b) False

9. Is 44.47 + 55.96 = 11.49
    a) True
    b) False

10. Is 33.35 + 42.2 + 10.33 = 105.88
    a) False
    b) True

11. Is 38.91 + 49.08 - 12.55 = 74.44
    a) False
    b) True

12. Is 36.13 + 45.64 = 81.77
    a) True
    b) False

13. Is 33.35 + 42.2 = 6.85
    a) False
    b) True

14. Is 66.28 - 52.81 = 10.47
    a) False
    b) True

15. Is 25 - 19.45 = 5.55
    a) True
    b) False

16. Is 33.35 + 42.2 = 8.85
    a) True
    b) False

17. Is 16.67 + 21.56 = 58.23
    a) False
    b) True

18. Is 52.81 + 66.28 + 18.1 = 137.19
    a) True
    b) False

19. Is 27.79 + 35.32 - 8.11 = 55
    a) True
    b) False

20. Is 25.01 + 31.88 + 7 = 83.89
    a) False
    b) True

21. Is 44.47 + 55.96 = 8.49
    a) False
    b) True

22. Is 36.13 + 45.64 - 11.44 = 67.33
    a) False
    b) True

23. Is 38.91 + 49.08 = 97.99
    a) False
    b) True

24. Is 44.47 + 55.96 = 130.43
    a) False
    b) True

25. Is 31.88 - 25.01 = 6.87
    a) True
    b) False

26. Is 27.79 + 35.32 + 8.11 = 71.22
    a) True
    b) False

27. Is 16.67 + 21.56 - 3.67 = 32.56
    a) False
    b) True

28. Is 30.57 + 38.76 + 9.22 = 88.55
    a) False
    b) True

29. Is 22.23 + 28.44 + 5.89 = 56.56
    a) True
    b) False

30. Is 30.57 + 38.76 = 79.33
    a) False
    b) True

Copyright - 101Minute.com

31. Is 47.25 + 59.4 + 15.88 = 132.53
    a) False
    b) True

32. Is 31.88 - 25.01 = 4.87
    a) False
    b) True

33. Is 25.01 + 31.88 - 7 = 47.89
    a) False
    b) True

34. Is 27.79 + 35.32 = 63.11
    a) True
    b) False

35. Is 52.81 + 66.28 = 119.09
    a) True
    b) False

36. Is 41.69 + 52.52 - 13.66 = 78.55
    a) False
    b) True

37. Is 50.03 + 62.84 - 16.99 = 95.88
    a) True
    b) False

38. Is 41.69 + 52.52 - 13.66 = 80.55
    a) True
    b) False

39. Is 19.45 + 25 + 4.78 = 79.23
    a) False
    b) True

40. Is 27.79 + 35.32 = 7.53
    a) True
    b) False

44.   ADD AND SUBTRACT DECIMAL NUMBERS (WORD PROBLEMS)

1. Paul's family prepared salsa over the weekend. If he prepared 260.50 grams of salsa and his father prepared 378.75 grams, how much salsa did they prepare altogether?

2. Kevin drove from San Francisco to Phoenix. He made a stopover at 355.75 miles. If the distance between San Francisco and Phoenix is 744.50 miles. How many miles did he need to cover to reach Phoenix after the stopover?

3. Liz spent a total $890.46 during her summer vacations at Orlando. She spent $225.25 on food. She spent another $435.60 on hotel rooms. How much did she spend on other stuff?
    a) 229.61
    b) 230.61
    c) 228.51
    d) 231.71

4. After the party, Tom calculated the money which he spent on food and drinks. If he spent $37.90 on food and $11.95 on drinks. How much did he spend in total?

5. Joe invited 5 friends on his birthday and ordered 2 varieties of pizza - cheese and peperoni. He spent $44.69 in total. Cost of cheese pizza was $13.95. Find the cost of peperoni pizza.

6. Joe's dad gave him $50.75 to buy gifts. He spent $39.90 to buy 4 gift items. How much money was he have left?

7. Annie spent $89.54 on shirts. She spent $34.71 more on pants than she spent on shirts. How much money did she spent to buy pants?

8. A builder paid $173.25 to buy cement on Monday. He paid $142.56 more on Tuesday. How much did he pay in total on Monday and Tuesday?

9. A building is 56.7 feet high. The builder is adding 5.25 feet antenna at the top of the building. Find the total length of the building after antenna is installed on the building?

10. Greg had $129.90 dollars in his wallet. He spent $79.48 dollars to buy a jacket, and $15.60 dollars to buy a shirt. How many dollars did Greg have left?

11. Cathy bought 12 crayons for $15.24. Mary bought 12 crayons for $16.75 from other shop. How much did Mary pay more than Cathy?

12. Steve bought a roll of ribbon. There were 9.5 meters of ribbon on the roll. Steve used 6.2 meters of ribbon to pack the gifts. How much ribbon is left on the roll?

13. Annie bought 2.50 lbs. flour. She also bought 1.50 lbs. sugar. Calculate the total weight of flour and sugar?

14. Mike spent $78.75 on pizza on his birthday. He spent $8.00 less on drinks than he spent on pizza. How much money did he spent on drinks?

15. To paint his home, Mike hired couple of painters. They bought 4.42 gallons of paint to add to the existing 6.50 gallons of paint they already had, how much paint did they have in total?

16. Annie spent $390.45 on her jewelry on Christmas. She also spent $270.32 to buy toys for her daughter and son. How much money did she spend on Christmas?

17. Mr. Paul traveled 250.50 miles by sea. He drove 150.75 miles by road. How many miles did he travel in total?
    a) 401.25
    b) 402.25
    c) 400.15
    d) 403.35

18. Beth bought t-shirts, and pants during her trip to India. She spent $247.50 on t-shirts. She spent $46.25 more on pants than she spent on t-shirts. How much money did she spent on pants?
    a) 293.75
    b) 294.75
    c) 292.65
    d) 295.85

19. Steve needs 18.50 feet of rope to make a swing. He already has 7.85 feet of rope at home. How much rope does he need to buy more?

20. Joe's dad was very sick last week. He gave $54.67 to the pharmacy to buy medicines. Pharmacist gave him $5.02 back in change. How much money did he pay to buy the medicines?

ANSWERS KEY

1.Fraction Concepts	2.Idenitfy Equal Fractions	3. Fractions (Word Problems)
1. 1/6	1. 8/18	1. 12 8/9
2. 2/23	2. 4/22	2. 3/4
3. 11/13	3. 9/15	3. 8/9
4. 13/15	4. 3/5	4. 9 5/6
5. 7/20	5. 12/27	5. 3/7
6. 12/23	6. 6/21	6. 1/5
7. 9/20	7. 2/11	7. 6/11
8. 3/10	8. 6/10	8. 1/4
9. 5/8	9. 5/7	9. 4/5
10. 27/50	10. 3/9	10. 2/5
11. 3/8	11. 1/3	11. 3/7
12. 9/17	12. 6/14	12. 5/28
13. 5/12	13. 2/3	13. 3 2/3
14. 11/20	14. 3/7	14. 8/9
15. 17/25	15. 15/27	15. 5/8
16. 5/24	16. 4/3	16. 9 1/4
17. 7/24	17. 5/9	17. 5/9
18. 12/25	18. 2/6	18. 9 1/4
19. 8/15	19. 4/9	19. 12 1/12
20. 12/25	20. 10/14	20. 12 8/9
	21. 1/6	
	22. 9/21	
	23. 10/18	
	24. 6/9	
	25. 4/14	
	26. 8/6	
	27. 15/21	
	28. 4/6	
	29. 12/9	
	30. 2/7	

Copyright - 101Minute.com

4.Write Fractions in Order	5.Find The Smallest and Largest Fractions	6.Fractions Patterns and Sequence
1. 4/7 is the smallest frac.	1. 6/3	1. False
1. 4/5 is the middle frac.	2. 5/2	2. 5/17
1. 4/2 is the greatest frac.	3. 6/3	3. 5/17
2. True	4. 7/2	4. 40/20
3. True	5. 6/4	5. 9/10
4. True	6. 34/4	6. True
5. True	7. 6/5	7. False
6. True	8. 205/5	8. 9/11
7. True	9. 3/1	9. 41/17
8. True	10. 6/15	10. 11/17
9. True	11. 6/5	11. True
10. True	12. 1/2	12. True
12. 1/9 is the smallest franc.	13. 101/2	13. 400/20
12. 3/9 is the middle frac.	14. 41/4	14. True
12. 5/9 is the greatest frac.	15. 9/2	15. 12/10
13. 2/7 is the smallest frac.	16. 19/9	16. 10/10
13. 2/6 is the middle frac.	17. 31/2	17. False
13. 2/5 is the greatest frac.	18. 17/7	18. True
14. 2/7 is the smallest frac.	19. 54/3	19. False
14. 3/7 is the middle frac.	20. 7/2	20. True
14. 4/7 is the greatest frac.	21. 7/3	
15. True	22. 1/2	
16. True	23. 19/9	
17. 1/5 is the smallest frac.	24. 7/3	
17. 4/5 is the middle frac.	25. 31/2	
17. 5/5 is the greatest frac.	26. 205/5	
18. True	27. 101/2	
19. 3/7 is the smallest frac.	28. 9/2	
19. 3/6 is the middle frac.	29. 7/3	
19. 3/5 is the greatest frac.	30. 8/3	
20. True	31. 5/2	
21. True	32. 18/2	
22. True	33. 3/1	
23. True	34. 103/3	
24. 3/8 is the smallest frac.	35. 5/3	
24. 3/6 is the middle frac.	36. 9/2	
24. 3/4 is the greatest frac.	37. 17/2	
25. True	38. 4/3	
26. True	39. 34/4	
27. 2/10 is the smallest frac.	40. 101/2	
27. 3/10 is the middle frac.		
27. 4/10 is the greatest frac.		
28. True		

Copyright - 101Minute.com

7.Add and Subtract Simple Fractions	8.Fractions Concepts (Missing Numbers)	9.Compare Simple Fractions
1. 5/21	1. 2/3	1. >
2. 1/32	2. 1	2. <
3. 21/29	3. 11/7	3. =
4. 1/41	4. 1/2	4. =
5. 19/28	5. 5/6	5. <
6. 1/37	6. 4/5	6. =
7. 7/22	7. 7/16	7. <
8. 5/31	8. 7/8	8. =
9. 1/10	9. 2/13	9. =
10. 1/33	10. 3/26	10. <
11. 13/25	11. 3/5	11. >
12. 11/24	12. 11/7	12. =
13. 1/39	13. 3/5	13. <
14. 1/36	14. 11/12	14. >
15. 1/40	15. 5	15. =
16. 3/20	16. 3/2	16. >
17. 9/23	17. 11/12	17. <
18. 1/38	18. 7/16	18. >
19. 1/44	19. 11/18	19. >
20. 1/35	20. 3/34	20. >
21. 1/43	21. 3/5	21. <
22. 1/34	22. 5	22. =
23. 17/27	23. 1	23. >
24. 15/26	24. 1	24. >
25. 1/42	25. 5/6	25. =
	26. 1/2	26. <
	27. 2/13	27. =
	28. 3/8	28. <
	29. 11/18	29. >
	30. 3/2	30. <
	31. 1/2	
	32. 4/5	
	33. 3/5	
	34. 5/2	
	35. 5/6	
	36. 41/18	
	37. 3/7	
	38. 3/5	
	39. 5/2	
	40. 1/2	

10.Compare Negative and Positive Fractions	11.Add and Subtract Mixed Numbers having Same Denominators	12.Add and Subtract Mixed Numbers
1. >	1. 4	1. 31/32
2. <	2. 1/43	2. 39/40
3. >	3. 1/3	3. 2/41
4. <	4. 2/5	4. 13/45
5. False	5. 7/3	5. 15/16
6. >	6. 2	6. 1/11
7. >	7. 3/20	7. 1 1/36
8. >	8. 1/34	8. 5 5/6
9. >	9. 1	9. 1/10
10. True	10. 1/42	10. 3 1/22
11. >	11. 11/24	11. 2 9/14
12. >	12. 4 1/4	12. 2 20/21
13. =	13. 2 3/5	13. 1 1/18
14. >	14. 1/32	14. 1/7
15. >	15. 1/4	15. 10 4/13
16. >	16. 15/26	16. 1 1/20
17. >	17. 1/10	17. 1/36
18. =	18. 3	18. 3 3/20
19. >	19. 1/44	19. 4 16/25
20. <	20. 1/40	20. 2 5/8
21. >	21. 2	21. 2 1/2
22. <	22. 1/37	22. 3
23. <	23. 1/38	23. 3 23/25
24. >	24. 1	24. 1/32
25. >	25. 19/28	25. 2 1/6
26. >	26. 1/2	
27. >	27. 2	
28. <	28. 7/22	
29. <	29. 5/3	
30. >	30. 10/3	
31. <	31. 1/2	
32. <	32. 1/3	
33. =	33. 17/27	
34. >	34. 5/31	
35. >	35. 5	
36. >	36. 5/21	
37. =	37. 1/33	
38. <	38. 1/35	
39. <	39. 5	
40. <	40. 21/29	

Copyright - 101Minute.com

13.Add and Subtract Fractions (True or False)	14.Add and Subtract up to Three Fractions having Same Denominators	15. Add and Subtract up to Three Fractions having Different Denominators
1. True	1. 45/88	1. 10 1/10
2. False	2. 51/98	2. 2 2/3
3. False	3. 36/73	3. 8 5/6
4. False	4. 9/28	4. 1 8/15
5. True	5. 18/43	5. 10 1/6
6. False	6. 27/58	6. 3 1/5
7. False	7. 11/21	7. 2 3/4
8. True	8. 33/68	8. 1 7/9
9. True	9. 25/36	9. 1 1/66
10. False	10. 1/2	10. 1 7/8
11. False	11. 7/13	11. -29/90
12. True	12. 42/83	12. 26/10
13. True	13. 7/16	13. -1/2
14. True	14. 15/38	14. 1 5/7
15. True	15. 8/15	15. 1 19/36
16. True	16. 22/41	16. 3 2/63
17. True	17. 43/81	17. 6 1/10
18. True	18. 4/11	18. 4 1/66
19. False	19. 13/24	19. 11 1/10
20. True	20. 16/31	20. 4 2/3
21. True	21. 10/21	21. 11 5/6
22. True	22. 6/23	22. 2 8/15
23. True	23. 24/53	23. 11 1/6
24. False	24. 33/68	24. 6 1/5
25. True	25 25/36	25. 3 3/4
26. True		
27. False		
28. False		

16.Add and Subtract 3 or more Fractions and Mixed Numbers having Same Denominators (Word Problems)	17.Add and Subtract Fractions (Word Problems)	18.Simple Fractions (Mixed Problems)
1. 1 13/16	1. 1/3	1. 3 miles
2. 1 11/14	2. 12	2. 80
3. 1 1/2	3. 4 2/3	3. 60 years
4. 1 7/8	4. 1 4/5	4. 1/3 mile
5. 1 23/26	5. 7/3	5. 2/3
6. 1 25/28	6. 5	6. 2/3 mile
7. 1 17/46	7. 11/5	7. 2/3
8. 1 1/5	8. 2	8. 5/6 miles
9. 1 5/6	9. 8	9. 10 years
10. 1 5/8	10. 11/12	10. 20
11. 31/36	11. 1	11.20
12. 1 17/20	12. 2 3/16	
13. 1 9/10	13. 1	
14. 1 7/10	14. 1	
15. 1 3/4	15. 1/4	
16. 1 25/28	16. 3	
17. 43/48	17. 2	
18. 29/34	18. 1/3	
19. 27/32	19. 3/5	
20. 1 19/22	20. 2	
	21. 5/3	
	22. 2/3	
	23. 2 3/5	
	24. 2	

19.Multiply Fractions and Whole Numbers (True or False)	20.Multiply Fractions by whole 1 or 2 Digit Numbers	21.Compare and Balance the Product of Two Fractions
1. True	1. 2 1/4	1. True
2. True	2. 20 5/8	2. True
3. False	3. 7 1/12	3. True
4. True	4. 3 3/4	4. False
5. False	5. 1 1/4`	5. False
6. False	6. 4 19/24	6. False
7. True	7. 2 21/52	7. True
8. True	8. 4 14/19	8. False
9. True	9. 3 15/16	9. False
10. True	10. 4	10. True
11. False	11. 9 7/17	11. True
12. True	12. 8 1/3	12. True
13. False	13. 22 8/11	13. True
14. True	14. 2 3/8	14. False
15. False	15. 11 23/32	15. True
16. False	16. 7 4/23	16. True
17. False	17. 2 2/5	17. False
18. True	18. 8 4/7	18. False
19. True	19. 18 6/13	19. True
20. True	20. 4	20. False
21. False	21. 1 2/3	21. False
22. True	22. 16 1/4	22. True
23. True	23. 14	23. True
24. False	24. 9 6/11	24. True
25. False	25. 11 19/21	25. True
26. True		26. True
27. True		27. False
28. True		28. True

22. Compare Fractions with Whole Number (True or False)	23. Multiply 2 Fractions	24. Multiply 2 Fractions (True or False)
1. True	1. 6 3/32	1. False
2. False	2. 97 1/17	2. True
3. False	3. 6 12/25	3. True
4. False	4. 5 5/56	4. False
5. True	5. 62 4/13	5. True
6. True	6. 6 4/21	6. False
7. False	7. 6 3/4	7. False
8. False	8. 5 275/512	8. True
9. True	9. 6 8/29	9. True
10. False	10. 6 564/841	10. True
11. False	11. 3 33/49	11. True
12. False	12. 53 1/3	12. False
13. True	13. 4 41/96	13. True
14. True	14. 3 59/72	14. True
15. False	15. 17 1/2	15. False
16. False	16. 5 6/7	16. True
17. True	17. 6 13/80	17. False
18. True	18. 3 3/8	18. False
19. True	19. 3 117/121	19. False
20. False	20. 1	20. False
21. True	21. 3 71/128	21. True
22. True	22. 101 17/27	22. True
23. False	23. 5 1/3	23. True
24. False	24. 19 4/9	24. True
25. False	25. 3 37/81	25. True
26. True		26. True
27. False		27. False
28. True		28. True
29. True		
30. True		
31. True		
32. True		
33. False		
34. False		
35. False		
36. True		
37. True		
38. False		
39. True		
40. True		

25. Fractions Problems (Word Problems)	26. Multiply up to 3 Fractions and Answer in Mixed Number	27. Divide Fractions – Fraction by Fraction
1. 7 1/12	1. 2 29/32	1. 5/6
2. 16 ¼	2. 1 9/16	2. 1/2
3. 1 1/4	3. 15/16	3. 1/2
4. 4	4. 1/8	4. 3/4
5. 14	5. 10 3/4	5. 4/5
6. 20 5/8	6. 5 5/8	6. 6/7
7. 1	7. 1 5/6	7. 3/4
8. 8 4/7	8. 1 3/32	8. 1/2
9. 11 23/32	9. 4 7/32	9. 2/3
10. 2 1/4	10. 11 7/8	10. 3/4
11. 18 6/13	11. 5 15/32	11. 6/7
12. 8 1/3	12. 3 15/16	12. 2/3
13. 3 3/4	13. 27/200	13. 1/2
14. 3 15/16	14. 7 1/4	14. 5/6
15. 22 8/11	15. 1 13/32	15. 4/5
16. 4	16. 1/18	16. 2
17. 5	17. 3/50	17. 5/6
	18. 7 21/32	18. 3/4
	19. 5/8	19. 4/5
	20. 1 7/10	20. 7/8
	21. 13/42	21. 8/9
	22. 1 1/24	22. 2/3
	23. 2 17/72	23. 5/6
	24. 2 11/18	24. 9/10
	25. 2 1/16	25. 4/5

28.Divide Fractions – Fraction and Whole Number	29.Compare Fractions Division (True or False)	30.Divide Fractions (True or False)
1. 1/6	1. False	1. True
2. 12	2. False	2. False
3. 1/12	3. True	3. True
4. 1/9	4. True	4. False
5. 1/33	5. True	5. False
6. False	6. True	6. False
7. 12	7. True	7. True
8. 1/12	8. True	8. True
9. 1/18	9. True	9. False
10. 1/15	10. True	10. True
11. 20	11. False	11. True
12. False	12. True	12. True
13. 1/18	13. True	13. False
14. 1/66	14. True	14. True
15. 15	15. True	15. False
16. True	16. True	16. False
17. 42	17. True	17. False
18. True	18. False	18. True
19. 20	19. False	19. False
20. 12	20. False	20. False
21. 1/6	21. True	21. False
22. False	22. True	22. False
23. 1/9	23. True	23. True
24. 1/18	24. True	24. False
25. 42	25. True	25. True
26. 1/24		26. False
27. 1/50		27. False
28. False		28. True
29. 1/15		29. False
30. 1/9		30. False
31. True		31. False
32. True		32. False
33. 30		33. False
34. 1/15		34. True
35. True		35. False
36. True		36. False
37. 1/50		37. True
38. 35		38. True
39. 7/3		39. False
40. 1/9		40. False

Copyright - 101Minute.com

31.Divide Whole Numbers by Fractions	32.Divide Whole Numbers by Mixed Number	33.Divide Fractions (Word Problems)
1. 8	1. 23/40	1. 15
2. 18	2. 64/85	2. 6
3. 36	3. 29/55	3. 14
4. 20	4. 1 1/18	4. 18
5. 28	5. 88/225	5. 1/3
6. 24	6. 2	6. 25
7. 30	7. 1 9/95	7. 1/3
8. 12	8. 2 2/7	8. 15
9. 14	9. 48/55	9. 25
10. 12	10. 1 1/3	10. 25
11. 36	11. 1 3/13	11. 9
12. 28	12. 11/15	12. 20
13. 20	13. 17/25	13. 15
14. 16	14. 4/9	14. 1/4
15. 9	15. 2 7/10	15. 1/4
16. 24	16. 64/135	16. 20
17. 12	17. 1 13/15	17. 10
18. 15	18. 1/5	18. 6
19. 25	19. 16/45	19. 1/4
20. 24	20. 1 11/25	20. 30
21. 42	21. 24/25	
22. 10	22. 25/27	
23. 20	23. 9/50	
24. 9	24. 1 7/45	
25. 18	25. 1/4	
26. 16		
27. 6		
28. 8		
29. 30		
30. 12		
31. 30		
32. 25		
33. 15		
34. 12		
35. 18		
36. 14		
37. 20		
38. 24		
39. 42		
40. 15		

34. Conversion Between Decimal and Fraction	35. Rounding of Decimal Numbers	36. Compare and Balance Equations having Decimal Numbers and Fractions
1. 1 9/20	1. 0.804	1. True
2. 1 7/50	2. 4.47	2. False
3. 3.45	3. 0.13	3. True
4. 37/50	4. 0.03	4. True
5. 1.85	5. 1.61	5. False
6. 2.45	6. 0.12	6. True
7. 17/20	7. 0.7	7. True
8. 1.94	8. 1.76	8. False
9. 1.74	9. 4	9. True
10. 1.54	10. 0.042	10. True
11. 2.25	11. 0.367	11. False
12. 9/20	12. 0.045	12. True
13. 3.65	13. 1.744	13. True
14. 4.05	14. 0.442	14. False
15. 3.05	15. 0.437	15. True
16. 1 1/20	16. 0.3	16. True
17. 17/50	17. 1.852	17. False
18. 2 7/50	18. 1.57	18. True
19. 1.34	19. 3.26	19. True
20. 4.25	20. 0.3	20. True
21. 27/50	21. 0.355	21. True
22. 13/20	22. 0.036	22. True
23. 3.85	23. 1.8	23. True
24. 3.25	24. 1.552	24. True
25. 1 1/4	25. 1.39	25. False
26. 2.65	26. 0.049	26. False
27. 47/50	27. 0.4	27. True
28. 1.65	28. 0.426	28. True
29. 2.05	29. 0.01	29. False
30. 2.85	30. 1.32	

37. Decimal Numbers Problems (True or False)	38. Decimal Numbers Problems (Word Problems)	39. Add Decimal Numbers
1. True	1. 100	1. 204383.06
2. True	2. 4.59	2. 189335
3. False	3. 258.5	3. 422579.93
4. True	4. 390.1	4. 565536.5
5. True	5. 696.14	5. 415055.9
6. True	6. 8	6. 588108.59
7. True	7. .921	7. 264575.3
8. False	8. 3.68	8. 445152.02
9. True	9. 1.92	9. 129142.76
10. False	10. 60000	10. 648300.83
11. True	11. 23	11. 490296.2
12. True	12. 438.77	12. 723541.13
13. True	13. 40000	13. 53902.46
14. True	14. 345	14. 520392.32
15. False	15. 360	15. 640776.8
16. True	16. 22.5	16. 369911.72
17. False	17. 107.5	17. 731065.16
18. True	18. 12	18. 294671.42
19. True		19. 136666.79
20. True		20. 595632.62
21. True		21. 46378.43
22. True		22. 279623.36
23. False		23. 580584.56
24. True		24. 738589.19
25. True		25. 663348.89
26. False		26. 670872.92
27. False		27. 68950.52
28. True		28. 655824.86
29. True		29. 211907.09
		30. 354863.66
		31. 362387.69
		32. 121618.73
		33. 61426.49
		34. 196859.03
		35. 497820.23
		36. 573060.53
		37. 746113.22
		38. 339815.6
		39. 287147.39
		40. 437627.99

Copyright - 101Minute.com

40.Subtract Decimal Numbers	41.Multiple Operations using Decimal Numbers	42.Add and Subtract Three Decimal Numbers
1. 81219.15	1. 14.81	1. 78.5
2. 88427.07	2. 20.92	2. 105.3
3. 27159.75	3. 541.94	3. 72.3
4. 71308.26	4. 428.68	4. 93.3
5. 26258.76	5. 49.97	5. 108.3
6. 16347.87	6. 131.35	6. 74.7
7. 90229.05	7. 162.31	7. 99.3
8. 42476.58	8. 374.88	8. 114.3
9. 54189.45	9. 8.67	9. 104.5
10. 5535.99	10. 4.584	10. 48.3
11. 72209.25	11. 115.87	11. 75.3
12. 80318.16	12. 55.87	12. 151.3
13. 77615.19	13. 23.56	13. 78.3
14. 7337.97	14. 154.57	14. 146.1
15. 45179.55	15. 67.21	15. 45.3
16. 61397.37	16. 224.19	16. 119.4
17. 78516.18	17. 173.64	17. 54.3
18. 33466.68	18. 22.44	18. 73.3
19. 60496.38	19. 67.28	19. 109.7
20. 14545.89	20. 122.64	20. 112.6
21. 18149.85	21. 2.88	21. 66.3
22. 79417.17	22. 77.97	22. 187.7
23. 32565.69	23. 509.2	23. 57.3
24. 25357.77	24. 146.83	24. 111.3
25. 24456.78	25. 147.52	25. 60.3
26. 35268.66	26. 23.43	26. 19.7
27. 51486.48	27. 5.1325	27. 198.1
28. 9139.95	28. 99.23	28. 52.9
29. 34367.67	29. 13.06	29. 90.3
30. 41575.59	30. 177.79	30. 79.3
31. 50585.49	31. 11.06	31. 37.5
32. 8238.96	32. 192.95	32. 84.3
33. 62298.36	33. 224.8	33. 166.9
34. 68605.29	34. 94.24	34. 182.5
35. 44278.56	35. 63.97	35. 192.9
36. 17248.86	36. 139.09	36. 203.3
37. 36169.65	37. 56.97	37. 99.3
38. 69506.28	38. 328.48	38. 81.3
39. 43377.57	39. 130.47	39. 33.1
40. 52387.47	40. 554.88	40. 140.9

Copyright - 101Minute.com

43.Add and Subtract Decimal Numbers (True or False)	**44.Add and Subtract Decimal Numbers (Word Problems)**	
1. False	1. 639.25	
2. False	2. 388.75	
3. False	3. 229.61	
4. True	4. 49.85	
5. False	5. 30.74	
6. False	6. 10.85	
7. True	7. 124.25	
8. True	8. 315.81	
9. True	9. 61.95	
10. False	10. 34.82	
11. False	11. 1.51	
12. True	12. 3.3	
13. False	13. 4	
14. False	14. 70.75	
15. True	15. 10.92	
16. True	16. 660.77	
17. False	17. 401.25	
18. True	18. 293.75	
19. True	19. 10.65	
20. False	20. 49.65	
21. False		
22. False		
23. False		
24. False		
25. True		
26. True		
27. False		
28. False		
29. True		
30. False		
31. False		
32. False		
33. False		
34. True		
35. True		
36. False		
37. True		
38. True		
39. False		
40. True		

Copyright - 101Minute.com

101Minute.com

Welcome to 101Minute.com, a guide dedicated to help students excel academically.

We are focused on creating educational programs that help to enhance student's skills across various grades and subjects. Modules are designed per grade level that progressively enhances their skill and confidence each day.

Each subject category has several quizzes designed to assess student's mastery with the concept. By consistently devoting 101 minutes per week, students can demonstrate significant improvement.

We are committed to serving our student community by building effective tools and reward programs. We are open to receiving feedback on how we can improve to make this an even better experience for our students. Our goal is to create a fun and learning social educational environment for students, and reward them for their achievements.

Please visit us at 101Minute.com.

Practice 101 Minutes Weekly to Master Your Math Skills

101Minute.com Inc. (101Minute.com) does not allow to reproduce, duplicate, copy, sell, resell, exploit, distribute any contents or any portion of this book in any form print or written or electronic or digital form without written authorization by 101Minute.com.
101Minute.com has tried to correlate its contents to grade levels in general but it is neither certified nor approved by any state authority or school. State or school standards may vary or change time-to-time. It is user's responsibility to verify it before buying or using it to meet grade or age levels. 101Minute.com does not guarantee or take any responsibility in case of any difference or change in grade levels in a state or a school. 101Minute.com has tried its best to maintain a comprehensive set of questions and right answers. If any user notices or finds any mistake, please notify to 101Minute.com via email admin@101minute.com and we will try to correct it in the next version as soon as possible but we cannot commit to a timeline to make those changes or updates in future releases. 101Minute.com and the author don't take any responsibility and do not guarantee correct answer for each and every question or any wrong question in the practice sets, books and contents.

$$\frac{1}{2} \times \frac{1}{2} = \frac{1}{4}$$

$$\frac{1}{5} = 5\overline{)1.0}$$

Made in the USA
Middletown, DE
27 May 2020

96073051R00073